Restoring Our
Friendship with God

Zacchaeus Studies: Theology

General Editor: Monika Hellwig

Restoring Our Friendship with God

The Mystery of Redemption from Suffering and Sin

by

Carol Frances Jegen, BVM

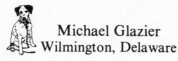
Michael Glazier
Wilmington, Delaware

About the Author

Carol Frances Jegen, BVM, is Professor of Religious Studies at Mundelein College in Chicago. A graduate of Marquette University, Dr. Jegen is the author of *Jesus the Peacemaker* and editor of *Mary According to Women*. She has served on the Advisory Board of the U.S. Catholic Bishops, the Board of Trustees of Catholic Theological Union, and the Board of Directors of the College Theology Society and of the Liturgical Conference.

First published in 1989 by Michael Glazier, Inc., 1935 West Fourth Street, Wilmington, Delaware 19805.

Library of Congress Cataloging-in-Publication Data

Jegen, Carol Frances.
    Restoring our friendship with God: the mystery of redemption from suffering and sin/by Carol Frances Jegen.
        p.   cm.—(Zacchaeus studies. Theology)
    Bibliography: p.
    ISBN: 0-89453-757-1
    1. Redemption.   2. Suffering—Religious aspects—Christianity.
3. Sin.   4. Catholic Church—Doctrines.   I. Title.   II. Series.
BT775.J44 1989
234'.3—dc20   88-82455
                                                        CIP

Cover Design by Maureen Daney
Typography by Phyllis Boyd LeVane
Printed in the United States of America by McNaughton & Gunn, Inc.

*In gratitude
to my friends
on earth
and in heaven*

Contents

Editor's Note

This series of short texts in doctrinal subjects is designed to offer introductory volumes accessible to any educated reader. Dealing with the central topics of Christian faith, the authors have set out to explain the theological interpretation of these topics in a Catholic context without assuming a professional theological training on the part of the reader.

We who have worked on the series hope that these books will serve well in college theology classes where they can be used either as a series or as individual introductory presentations leading to a deeper exploration of a particular topic. We also hope that these books will be widely used and useful in adult study circles, continuing education and RENEW programs, and will be picked up by casual browsers in bookstores. We want to serve the needs of any who are trying to understand more thoroughly the meaning of the Catholic faith and its relevance to the changing circumstances of our times.

Each author has endeavored to present the biblical foundation, the traditional development, the official church position and the contemporary theological discussion of the doctrine or topic in hand. Controversial questions are discussed within the context of the established teaching and the accepted theological interpretation.

We undertook the series in response to increasing interest among educated Catholics in issues arising in the contemporary church, doctrines that raise new questions in a contemporary setting, and teachings that now call for wider and deeper appreciation. To such people we offer these volumes, hoping that reading them may be a satisfying and heartening experience.

Monika K. Hellwig
Series Editor

Introduction

Redemption from suffering and sin is a central tenet of Christian faith. Today's eucharistic proclamation of the mystery of faith has resounded throughout the centuries: "Lord, by your cross and resurrection you have set us free. You are the Savior of the world." The recognized symbol for Christian faith is the cross, recalling the redeeming suffering and death of Jesus.

Theological probings into the mystery of redemption have been both helpful and misleading. Far too often, exaggerated notions of human sinfulness have crippled the vitality of Christian faith life. Sometimes, even in liturgical celebrations of God's overwhelmingly redeeming love in Jesus, one might wonder if the people of God were really redeemed, because of the ways some homilies and prayer texts continually emphasize the sinfulness of the worshippers.

Far more problematic is the distorted image of God which predominates whenever misunderstandings prevail regarding redemption from sin and suffering. Then God is seen sometimes as a demanding deity who sends all kinds of sufferings into human life in order to punish sinful people or to test their virtue. Often it is difficult to recognize such a god as the God of Jesus. This problem regarding God's image becomes acute if the impression is given that God demanded the crucifixion of Jesus in order to make amends for all the sins of the human family.

However, regardless of theological clarifications about the meaning of redemption from sin, the fact of human suffering persists with its many heartaches and questions. In the face of so much suffering, particularly on the part of good people and even little children, one must raise the question of God's goodness.

This present approach to the mystery of redemption from suffering and sin focuses on the even greater mystery of God's call to friendship, to an intimate sharing of life in time and in eternity. As indicated in the titles of each chapter, this study is a constant reminder that suffering and sin are mystery, because their meaning can be found only in the light of a loving God's wisdom.

In considering the mystery of human sufferings, chapter 1 begins to focus on Jesus' own experience of suffering in others' lives as well as his own. Chapter 2 begins to discuss the mystery of sin in relation to suffering, including some of the pastoral anguish caused by misunderstandings regarding human sinfulness.

Chapter 3, The Mystery of Jesus presents some of the theological developments regarding Jesus' universal salvific mission. The final chapter explores some aspects of the Church's life in the mystery of ongoing redemption. Particular emphasis is placed on the present challenges facing the Church. A biblical theology is interwoven throughout the entire study along with other contemporary theological insights.

Special gratitude goes to Mundelein College for rearranging my teaching schedule in order to complete this manuscript. But most of all, I am grateful to the many friends who have helped me understand something of the mystery of our friendship with God.

1

The Mystery of Suffering

The Human Predicament

Suffering is a reality in human life which continues to raise critical questions about the meaning and purpose of human existence. The reality of suffering also has raised critical questions about God. Because suffering is such a universal phenomenon throughtout human history, it is not surprising that questions about the meaning of suffering have been asked in all cultures and various explanations have been given.

Puzzlement and frustration abound when one examines theories of human error and culpability as remote and proximate causes of suffering. But far greater puzzlement and frustration develop when one begins to ponder divine omnipotence and wisdom and goodness in the face of relentless suffering in the entire human family. When one adds the well-known phrase "of the innocent," then the questions surrounding human suffering become almost overwhelming.

More than explanations of suffering have been attempted through the centuries. Ways and means to avoid and eliminate suffering are common in the history of the human family. When suffering enters human life, usually people are not too concerned about defining the experience. Sufferers know that suffering means something has happened to a person which causes pain or distress in some way. Usually the first response is to try to get rid of the suffering as fast as possible. Most people agree pain and distress are to be avoided at all costs. Furthermore in today's

13

technological society, the elimination of more and more human suffering is becoming a realizable goal, both from the standpoint of preventing and healing diseases and from the standpoint of averting massive suffering such as widespread hunger.

However, the possibility of preventing suffering through technological achievements must be considered alongside the possibility of causing more suffering, also through technological expertise. One has only to recall the unimaginable sufferings caused by holocaust ovens and by sophisticated torture and weapon systems developed in our own century to know that although the capability of preventing much suffering really exists through developments in modern technology, the opposite is also true. Particularly in the light of modern warfare with its implications for the cruel destruction of entire populations does the question of human suffering reach incalculable magnitude and intensity. Furthermore, especially in the light of modern technology does the question of suffering touch all of life, not just human life. Every living creature and the entire planet can be inflicted with suffering undreamt of in other periods of history.

Human suffering is more than physical pain. Who could even begin to list the many ways a person can suffer in mind and heart? The pain of loss, of separation, loneliness, rejection, betrayal, disappointment and frustration are some of the sufferings commonly and frequently experienced by most people. No wonder suffering continues to raise questions about the meaning and purpose of human existence. No wonder suffering continues to raise questions about God. What kind of a world did God create? Did it have to be this way? In the face of all the suffering in this world God created, can God possibly be good? And some would ask the further question, Does God exist?

When the experience of suffering raises the question of divine providence and goodness, then suffering can be considered more as a *mystery* to be probed rather than a *problem* to be solved. However, in shifting an approach from problem to mystery, it is extremely important to avoid thinking of mystery as an intellectual escape of some sort. Far too often the impression has been given that mystery in the theological sense is an easy substitute for the intellectual work demanded by the most critical questions. On the contrary, facing mystery theologically is an awesome intellectual challenge because mystery brings us into the realm of the divine.

Many people on hearing the word, mystery, probably think of a detective story, so often referred to simply as a mystery. If mystery is understood primarily in this detective context, then mystery and problem are somewhat synonymous. A mystery story is a problem solving challenge, something like a jigsaw puzzle, demanding careful observation to recognize clues which will indicate how the pieces fit together.

Perhaps one of the best examples of this problem solving approach to suffering can be found in the dialogues of the Book of Job, that literary masterpiece of the Hebrew Scriptures. Job's friends are tireless in their search for clues in Job's life which will explain his horrible predicament. When their manifold questions elicit no satisfactory answers from Job, the friends resort to making up clues by means of the false accusations leveled at him.

From Job's point of view, his friends' questions are meaningless and irrelevant because they do not pertain to his life experience. As the irrelevant questioning search for clues entrenches Job's friends in a problem-solving approach, Job is drawn ever more deeply into the mystery of God. Job's conviction intensifies that his suffering somehow belongs to the divine mystery.

Theologically speaking, mystery is a centuries-old way of referring to divine reality. Mystery means something, or better, someone is both concealed and revealed, unknown and known in human experience. When understood correctly, mystery is a positive, attractive word indicating there is always "more to discover." The "more to discover" aspect of theological mystery does have something in common with the detective story. But theological mystery goes far beyond the detective search. In theological mystery, discovery cannot be concluded as though a problem were finally solved. There is always more to discover when one approaches the reality of God.

Mystery always calls for reflection. Mystery by its very nature as pertaining to divine reality invites one to prayer. As one becomes more and more comfortable with a mystery approach to all of reality, one gradually sees more and more traces of divine love everywhere. One who is at home with mystery lives in a spirit of wonder and knows the joy of surprise, that special language of love. Particularly when one approaches suffering and even sin as mystery, can one find the transforming power of a loving God.

Although a mystery approach to suffering is quite different from a problem solving approach, mystery doesn't dismiss the validity and value of the human endeavor to avoid and eliminate as much suffering as possible. Quite the contrary, approaching suffering as mystery can give great impetus to human efforts focused on the prevention and healing of human hurt. The more one is attuned to the ways of a compassionate God, the more one is compelled to do something about the suffering members of the family of God.

Approaching suffering as mystery will also concentrate on the question of meaning, thereby touching the very heart of personal life and the core and center of human existence. Perhaps no one has contributed more understanding to the pivotal question of meaning in human life than the renowned psychiatrist, Victor Frankl. A survivor of the brutality characterizing the Jewish holocaust's concentration camps, Dr. Frankl highlights the crucial importance of meaning in human life, especially with respect to suffering. His classic work, *Man's Search for Meaning*, gives eloquent and profound testimony to the strength engendered in the human spirit when a person finds meaning and purpose in even the cruelest of suffering.

Another holocaust survivor, Elie Wiesel, poignantly raises the question of God in the midst of malicious suffering. Weisel's oft-repeated story of the young Jewish boy slowly dying on a gallows answers the question of God's whereabouts by locating God in that child's death agony. Weisel's account, like the story of Job, puts human suffering into the mystery of God. Or perhaps we should say, Weisel puts God in the mystery of human suffering.

A Christian Faith Perspective

From a Christian faith perspective, it is neither surprising nor new to affirm God's special presence in the mystery of human suffering. The Christian doctrine of incarnation makes the claim that in Jesus of Nazareth, God has irrevocably become human. In Jesus, the Word who is eternally with God, was made flesh. It is this same Jesus, Word made flesh, who really suffers throughout his life and finally dies the cruel death of crucifixion.

Throughout its history the Church has wrestled with the mystery of the divine and human in Jesus, especially with respect to suffering. One of the earliest attempts to resolve the issue resulted in denying that Jesus really suffered. Docetism, a name derived from the Greek word for an actor's mask, claimed that the humanity of Jesus was something like a mask enabling Jesus to give the appearance of suffering. But because Jesus was truly the Word made flesh, Docetists could not reconcile human suffering with a divine being. According to the Docetist position, the unity of the divine and human in Jesus made suffering impossible for him.

In refuting Docetism, the Church clearly affirmed that Jesus' true and genuine humanity meant Jesus really suffered. However, the strong influence of Greek philosophical thought resulted in various explanations to safeguard the unchangeableness and impassibility of Jesus' divinity. The God of the ancient Greek thought world could hardly suffer and still be God. Into the medieval period and beyond, carefully nuanced language was used in an attempt to reconcile the doctrine of incarnation with the actual sufferings of Jesus and with the immutability of God.

The question of freedom rose frequently in the theological probings into the mystery of Jesus' sufferings. Questions abounded regarding the freedom of God as Creator of a universe in which suffering exists, along with questions concerning Jesus' authentic human freedom in entering into and accepting the experience of human suffering.

Freedom questions sooner or later move one into the area of love, both human and divine. This probing into the relation between freedom and love helped make room for some of the contemporary approaches to the mystery of suffering. Today, theologians more attuned to a biblical theology do not hesitate to speak of a suffering Jesus, and even of a suffering God. Jürgen Moltmann's highly significant work entitled, *The Crucified God*, readily comes to mind in this context. Less well known is the French theologian, Francois Varillon whose study is entitled, *The Humility and Suffering of God.* From our twentieth century perspective, as we look back into the history of Christian faith life, we can say we have come from wrestling with a denial of a suffering Jesus to pondering an affirmation of a suffering God.

Latin America's liberation theology also makes very important contributions to the doctrinal development concerning the mystery of suffering. Very attuned to recent Christological emphases on the genuine humanness of Jesus and all that implies for human growth and maturing, liberation theologians have gained needed understanding of Jesus' suffering by relating Jesus' experience to the experience of their own suffering people. Jesus' reaction to suffering is seen more and more clearly in the light of suffering Christians today.

No matter what question of human life confronts Christians, the almost instinctive response of faith is to turn to the Jesus of the Gospels for some kind of wisdom and clarity. Granted, the Jesus of the Gospels will not give detailed answers about cultural and historical situations unknown in his lifetime. To expect such answers from the Gospel not only implies a facile problem-solving approach, but also denies Jesus' true humanness, at least indirectly. Jesus did not have some magical way of knowing human predicaments totally foreign to his own historical life situations. But invaluable wisdom regarding common human experience can be found in the Gospel. One such issue, perhaps the most mysterious one, is the reality of human suffering.

At this point in our present study, I want to suggest that we look carefully at one Gospel, the Gospel of Luke, from a particular point of view, namely, Jesus' approach to suffering. In so doing, we will constantly keep in mind that Jesus is the Word of God incarnate. Jesus helps us understand how God is expressed humanly among us. In other words, as contemporary Christians, drawing on the rich heritage of the Church's doctrinal development, once again we raise the critical question of human suffering and turn to Jesus for meaning. In Jesus we can find meaning according to the wisdom of God who has truly entered into human life, even into the mystery of suffering unto death.

Jesus' Approach to Suffering

The infancy narrative of the Lucan Gospel gives us the name for Mary's child. "Do not be afraid, Mary, for you have found favor with God. And behold, you will conceive in your womb and bear a son, and you shall call his name Jesus" (Lk 1:31). Mary was informed that her child would be known as "Yahweh saves," the Hebraic meaning for the name, Jesus. As a Jewish woman living in Roman occupied teritory, Mary was acutely aware of the dire need for Yahweh's saving action. The Lucan Magnificat gives some indication of the manifold sufferings of the people of Mary's time. The mighty on thrones were oppressing the lowly. People were hungry because the rich hoarded their wealth for themselves (Lk 1:52, 53). From the moment of his conception, Mary knew her son was destined to save people from their suffering.

Mary also knew quite early on in Jesus' life that he would suffer and she would share in those sufferings of her son. Simeon did not mince words when he spoke of Jesus' rejection and used the image of a piercing sword to describe Mary's sufferings (Lk 2:34, 35).

The infancy narrative ends with a story of acute suffering on the part of Mary and Joseph when Jesus was lost for three days during the passover celebration. This episode points ahead to the passion narrative wherein Mary would enter most fully into Jesus' sufferings.

The story of the loss and finding of Jesus in the temple helps the gospel reader understand that the infancy narrative keynotes the entire Gospel and already incorporates its major themes. Jesus enters the scene identified as "Yahweh saves." Just how Jesus would do this is not totally clear in this introductory section of the Gospel. It is clear that his mother would share in his mission, a theme which will be developed more extensively in chapter 4 of this study. The Lucan infancy narrative also proclaims that Jesus would know the suffering of rejection. And it is very clear from the setting of Jesus' birth that Jesus would know much human suffering by experience. According to Luke, Jesus was born poor, laid in a manger (Lk 2:7).

Before leaving the Lucan infancy narrative it is important to point out that an exceedingly rich theological motif is keynoted there, namely, the servant theology of Second Isaiah. Simeon refers to Jesus as "a light for revelation to the Gentiles, and for glory to thy people Israel" (Lk 2:32). The text is taken from the first servant song recorded in Isaiah, chapter 42. As the Gospel of Luke continues, another text from this first servant song is woven into two strategic episodes in Jesus' life, his baptism and his transfiguration. When Jesus is identified as the beloved Son, the chosen one (Lk 3:22; 9:35), the Lucan author, reflecting the faith of the early Christian community, is pointing to Jesus as the servant of Yahweh, that special intimate friend of God who was the prophet *par excellence*. Jesus identified himself in this way when he entered the Nazareth synagogue at the inauguration of his public ministry. "There was given to him the book of the prophet Isaiah. He opened the book and found the place where it was written,

> The Spirit of the Lord is upon me,
> because he has anointed me to
>   preach good news to the poor.
> He has sent me to proclaim release
>   to the captives
> and recovering of sight to the blind,
> to set at liberty those who are
>   oppressed,
> to proclaim the acceptable year of
>   the Lord (Lk 4:17, 18).

Although this text is not considered one of the four servant songs, it is clearly a text from the prophet-servant theology of the Isaian school.

In writing *Jesus the Peacemaker*, in the third chapter I illustrated the theological progression and continuity found in the four servant songs of Second Isaiah. Recalling that the fourth servant song is often referred to as the song of the suffering servant (Is 52:13—53:12), one can expect to find key insights in these songs with respect to an Hebraic approach to the mystery of human suffering. Such an approach would have been very familiar to Jesus. According to Isaian servant theology, a person who is touched profoundly by the Spirit of God is led to alleviate human sufferings of all kinds. This ministry draws the prophet servant ever more deeply into the mystery of suffering, never for its own sake, but always to heal and save the suffering people of God.

The Nazareth synagogue scene, in which Jesus identifies himself as servant of Yahweh, is a teaching scene. There Jesus proclaims the good news of God's saving power. This scene is also one of great suffering for Jesus. He experienced rejection, violent rejection, as his own townspeople tried to hurl him over the edge of a hill (Lk 4:28-30). What heartache Jesus must have known as he left Nazareth for Capernaum, there to continue his teaching.

When one considers Jesus' manifold actions in alleviating suffering, probably the first things that immediately come to mind are the numerous cures Jesus worked. Significantly, Luke's panoramic view of Jesus' healing ministry to the physically sick and handicapped is introduced by a reference to his teaching. In pondering Jesus' approach to suffering it is important to realize that Jesus the teacher was alleviating suffering, the suffering caused by ignorance, particularly the ignorance of God's goodness and love. As prophet-servant of Yahweh, Jesus was involved in healing every kind of human suffering. Ignorance is a universal cause of much human anguish. Jesus was keenly aware of that fact and spent himself in preaching and teaching the good news of God's saving love.

Whenever and wherever Jesus saw a suffering person, he moved immediately to do something about it. The Lucan stories of cures begin with a demoniac, thereby illustrating Jesus' power over human suffering at its deepest roots. The description of this man possessed with an unclean spirit includes that spirit's shrieking out in a loud voice. "Ah! What have you to do with us, Jesus of Nazareth? Have you come to destroy us? I know who you are, the Holy One of God." (Lk 4:34). Jesus' response is important to note carefully. "But Jesus rebuked him, saying, 'Be silent, and come out of him!' " (Lk 4:35). The demon obeyed.

In his recent penetrating study, *Suffering A Test of Theological*

Method, noted theologian Arthur McGill highlights the force of the demonic in our day. Commenting on the New Testament portrayal of Jesus, McGill emphasizes that Jesus is engaged with "energies of violation," demonic forces entangling and subjecting human beings.[1] McGill claims that in our times with its horrendous forces of destruction and death, "the demonic has replaced sin as the decisive form of evil, and therefore as the decisive arena for Christ's victory— or impotence,"[2]

In the Lucan Gospel before Jesus was led by the Spirit to teach in the Nazareth synagogue, he was led by that same Spirit into the desert to confront personally the power of the demonic. The significance of these early encounters in Jesus' life, both in the desert and in the Capernaum synagogue where he cured a man with an unclean spirit, must not be underestimated when one approaches human suffering as mystery. There is more to discover than meets the eye when one confronts the suffering which continually plagues the human family.

Some of the earliest letters to the Christian communities give evidence of an awareness of demonic forces at work in the struggles and sufferings of human existence. The Ephesians were reminded to "be strong in the Lord and in the strength of his might" because they were "not contending against flesh and blood, but against the principalities, against the powers, against the world rulers of this present darkness, against the spiritual hosts of wickedness in the heavenly places" (Eph 6:10, 12). The Colossians were taught that God disarmed "the principalities and powers" through the triumph of Christ's suffering and death on a cross (Col 2:14, 15). To speak of demonic forces in any age is to speak of a profoundly mysterious element about which we know very little with clarity and precision. But in the light of the New Testament, the power of the demonic cannot be ignored if one is to probe the mystery of human suffering from a Christian faith perspective.

---

[1]Arthur C. McGill, *Suffering, A Test of Theological Method* (Philadelphia: Westminster Press, 1982) p. 51.

[2]*Ibid.,* p. 52.

Immediately after Jesus cured the demoniac in the synagogue at Capernaum, the Lucan Gospel pictures him curing Simon's mother-in-law from a severe fever (Lk 4:38f). Then by evening, "all those who had any that were sick with various diseases brought them to him; and he laid his hands on every one of them and healed them" (Lk 4:40). One of the most important aspects of Jesus' approach to all these suffering people is his personal concern for each sufferer. Quite literally, each one received his personal touch. Another early healing story in Luke portrays Jesus curing a leper. Once again Jesus extended his hand and touched the leper personally (Lk 6:12f.).

A particular dimension to human suffering is highlighted in the next healing story, that of a paralyzed man. Aware of the keen human suffering of guilt, Jesus forgave the man's sins before he cured him of his paralysis (Lk 6:17f.). The relationship between suffering and sin is highly problematic and will be considered more extensively later in this study. Here the point of concern is Jesus' awareness of every kind of human suffering and his immediate, caring, personal response to the one who was in pain.

As the Lucan stories of cures continue throughout these early chapters of the Gospel, Jesus demonstrates a particular love for persons who not only knew the pains of various diseases, but who, like the leper, also knew the pains of social stigma and oppression. Jesus reached out to the son of a widow, a woman who knew the continual suffering caused by inequality according to law (Lk 7:11f); to a penitent women ostracized as a sinner (Lk 7:36f); to a little girl, one who must have already suffered from the automatic label of "inferior" simply because she wasn't a boy (Lk 8:40f.); to a hemorrahaging woman, who for twelve years had borne the stigma of being unclean (Lk 8:43f.). Jesus even responded to a Roman centurion's request, recognizing in that national enemy the broken heart of a man pleading for his servant's life (Lk 7:1f.). In all these episodes Jesus was manifesting a preferential option for the poor, for those who needed release from all sorts of afflictions, but even more importantly, needed assurance of their own dignity and self-worth.

Contemplating Jesus in each of these scenes of human suffering is a necessasry condition to understand his teachings which are interwoven with these stories. The beatitudes, part of Jesus' great discourse on the plain, are inserted after Luke depicts the large crowd of people who came to hear Jesus and "be healed of their diseases" (Lk 6:17). The Lucan beatitudes are reduced to four. Those who are poor, who hunger, who are weeping, who are ostracized and insulted like the prophets are called blest by Jesus (Lk 6:20f.). These are the suffering persons who need and will receive God's special compassionate love.

Chapter 6 also includes two episodes of suffering which are intertwined with sabbath regulation problems. The suffering of human hunger and the suffering of a withered hand provide occasions for Jesus to teach as well as to heal. One of the greatest sufferings of his people at that time was excessive legalism on the part of many religious leaders. Jesus was continually confronting this abusive religious stance, not only because it caused people great physical suffering, but even more tragically caused untold suffering of mind and heart. The worst part about religious legalism, then and now, is the way in which it distorts one's understanding of God, thereby continually undermining one's interior peace. The god of religious legalism is an exacting, demanding, punishing god. Such a god is a far cry from the covenant God of loving kindness and fidelity.

The celebration of sabbath was meant to be a joyful celebration of human life, of persons freed from bondage because of God's faithful love. What a horrendous distortion to so misinterpret the law as to prevent the alleviation of human suffering because of so-called sabbath observance. Jesus' teaching on the meaning of sabbath accompanied his sabbath cures of a man with a withered hand (Lk 6:6f.); of a pathetically stooped woman (Lk 13:10f.);of a man suffering from dropsy (Lk 14:1f.). Jesus also clarified some grave misconceptions about actions needed to alleviate hunger (Lk 6:1f.).

Particularly in this context of sabbath healing and teaching did Jesus suffer mounting opposition and hostility on the part of many religious leaders. Such antagonism never prevented Jesus from doing all he could to undo the suffering he confronted on the sabbath and also the anguish caused by the terrible misinterpretations of the sabbath's meaning.

In considering Jesus' approach to suffering, it is important to realize Jesus' great care in preventing increased suffering, caused by attitudes and actions of retaliation and revenge. Immediately after the beatitudes and contrasting woes are proclaimed in chapter 6 of the Lucan Gospel, Jesus' amazing doctrine on love of enemies is presented by means of startling examples. "Love your enemies, do good to those that hate you, bless those who curse you, pray for those who abuse you. To him who strikes you on the cheek, offer the other also; and from him who takes away your cloak do not withhold your coat as well. Give to everyone who begs from you; and of him who takes away your goods do not ask them again" (Lk 6:27-30).

One of the clearest episodes illustrating Jesus' teaching on love of enemies is that of the Samaritan's lack of hospitality (Lk 9:51f.). As Jesus began his journey toward Jerusalem, a certain Samaritan town refused to welcome him. The reason was clear and simple. Jesus was on his way to Jerusalem, that city of Judea which symbolized for the Samaritans all the animosity and rivalry which had mounted through the years because Samaritan background, customs and beliefs were different from those of their Judean neighbors. Furthermore, those Samaritan townspeople probably knew Jesus was a Galilean Jew, one more reason for refusing hospitality.

The reaction of the disciples James and John was clear evidence they had not taken to heart Jesus' teaching on love of enemies. Those two disciples suggested calling down fire from heaven to destroy the entire town, all of whom, children included, were perceived as enemies. Jesus would have none of it. His mission was to mitigate and alleviate suffering, not to increase it. The Lucan writer describes Jesus' immediate, decisive response to the two disciples' suggestion for violent reprisal. "He turned and rebuked them" (Lk 9:55).

This episode with Samaritan villagers is helpful in setting the context for the well-known parable of the good Samaritan which follows in the next chapter (Lk 10:25f.). This beautiful story of compassion for a suffering person is told in response to a question, "And who is my neighbor?" The story is well known. It is a story of great surprise.

If the logic of James and John were followed regarding the cruel retaliating destruction of the Samaritan villagers, then the Samaritan traveler in this parable probably would have finished off the malicious beatings of the robbers. The man lying on the ground "half dead" would have been beaten by the Samaritan until he died.

But this Samaritan, this perceived enemy, was moved to pity for the suffering traveler. What extraordinary care and concern he exerted, not only for the immediate relief of the wounded man, but for his recovery. The Samaritan made sure the innkeeper would look after the traveler. All added expenses were taken care of. At the conclusion of the parable, Jesus urged his hearers, "Go and do likewise" (Lk 10:37).

Three other famous parables, unique to the Lucan Gospel, graphically portray Jesus' approach to suffering. The introductory remarks preceding the parables establish their context (Lk 15:1f.). Tax collectors and sinners had gathered around Jesus, a situation which was distasteful to several of the religious leaders. Jesus wisely used the occasion to teach about his response to those who know suffering caused by personal sin.

In the first two parables a person suffering from sin is described as something that is lost. A lost sheep and a lost coin are indeed novel ways to describe something of the pain one undergoes in experiencing the alienation and isolation from community which sin eventually causes.

Both parables also highlight the apparent insignificance and inferiority often felt by one who is alienated. After all, what is one lost sheep when the shepherd had ninety-nine others? One coin, although probably quite significant to the woman who searches diligently, is nevertheless contrasted with nine others.

The shepherd and the woman, both images of the compassionate God of Jesus, are tireless in their searching, regardless of the inconvenience and anxiety they both suffer. The shepherd and the woman really care about their lost sheep and lost coin. Both parables end on a note of joy and community celebration when the lost has been found. The festive celebration theme is intensified in the third parable which more dramatically brings the themes of alienation and isolation directly into a human context. No longer are the lost articles a sheep and a coin, but a son who is really responsible for his deplorable condition.

The excitement and initiative of the father who runs to embrace his son is a climactic scene in this third parable. Then this exuberant father plans to celebrate the boy's return to his family. How skillfully this parable highlights Jesus' message of complete forgiveness by contrasting the bargaining attitude of the elder son who suffers from a lack of love for his wayward brother. The father, a man who loves both his sons, does all he can to bring them out of their situations of suffering caused by selfishness in one form or another. This father, another image of the God of Jesus, does not inflict more suffering by means of scoldings and punishments. This father overwhelms his suffering children with compassionate love.

All these Lucan texts among others portray Jesus as a person very familiar with human suffering. As the infancy narrative indicated, Jesus was continually involved in saving people from every kind of human suffering and distress—physical, psychological, social and spiritual. Jesus' teachings corrresponded with his actions, not only with respect to alleviating suffering, but also with reference to the prevention of additional suffering from actions of retaliation and revenge. Along the way, Jesus entered into the suffering of his people, particularly Israel's prophets who knew so much resistance, hostility and rejection. Such opposition led Jesus into the mystery of suffering unto death.

Jesus Suffers Unto Death

One helpful way to approach the entire Lucan passion narrative is to begin with the question Jesus asked the two disciples on the way to Emmaus: "Was it not necessary that the Christ should suffer these things and enter into his glory?" (Lk 24:26). Those two disciples were completely disillusioned. They were really undone by the mystery of suffering. From their point of view, it was obvious they had been misled. Jesus, "a prophet mighty in deed and word before God and all the people" (Lk 24:19), had really suffered the criminal's death penalty of crucifixion. As far as those two disciples could see, all the hopes of Israel's deliverance from Roman bondage had been dashed to the ground.

According to the Emmaus account, Jesus used the Hebrew Scriptures familiar to those two distraught travelers to interpret what had happened to himself. Jesus began with Moses and all the prophets (Lk 24:27). Surely a major focus must have been the Isaian prophet who saw suffering not without hope nor without meaning for the future. Jesus' teachings had a transforming effect on those Emmaus disciples. "Their eyes were opened and they recognized him" when "he took the bread and blessed, and broke it, and gave it to them" (Lk 24: 31, 30).

The Emmaus story presents the risen Jesus in a eucharistic context, compassionately explaining that the Messiah must suffer. As the Lucan Gospel relates the account of Jesus' passion, all aspects of human suffering are included. A passover motif introduces the tragic events with specific reference to the lamb which had to be sacrificed (Lk 22:1, 7f.). When Jesus sat at the passover table with his apostles, his first remarks resonate with his Emmaus question about the suffering of the Messiah. At that last supper before his crucifixion, Jesus remarked, "I have earnestly desired to eat this passover with you before I suffer" (Lk 22:15).

In some ways, all the aspects of Jesus' approach to suffering which we have considered thus far in the Gospel of Luke are found in the passion narrative. Right from the beginning Luke focuses on demonic power when he states that "Satan entered into Judas called Iscariot" (Lk 22:3). When Jesus warned Peter about his pending denial, again demonic power is referred to. "Simon, Simon, behold, Satan demanded to have you, that he might sift you like wheat, but I have prayed for you that your faith may not fail" (Lk 22:31, 32).

How significant that Jesus commented on the power of his own prayer in the context of demonic power. A little later, both before and after his own agony in the garden, Jesus urged his disciples to pray that they would not enter into temptation.

No other gospel account portrays the suffering of Jesus' agony in more vivid terms than does the Gospel of Luke who alone tells us, "his sweat became like great drops of blood falling down upon the ground" (Lk 22:44). It is well nigh impossible to imagine, much less describe the excruciating suffering of Jesus' passion. Not only the physical torment, but the psychological sufferings of ingratitude; mockery; false accusations; betrayal, denial and abandonment by friends all added to the overwhelming sufferings Jesus experienced. As one convicted to a criminal's death, Jesus knew social stigma at its worst. And who could even attempt to fathom his spiritual suffering of apparent abandonment by God?

Even in the midst of all this suffering, Jesus continued to cure and to comfort those in need. Not only was the slave's right ear healed (Lk 22:51), but Jesus once again stopped more retaliating violence with his stark command, "No more of this!" (Lk 22:51). Jesus took time to respond to the women who wept for him (Lk 23:27f.). He promised a dying criminal an immediate entry into paradise (Lk 23:43).

Jesus' forgiving spirit during his passion is highlighted in a particular way in the Lucan Gospel. Only Luke mentions Jesus' words, "Father, forgive them; for they know not what they do" (Lk 23:34). Luke also give more than a clue to the source of strength which sustained Jesus as he suffered unto death. Jesus trusted God to the end. He finally cried out with a loud voice before he breathed his last breath, "Father, into thy hands I commit my spirit" (Lk 23:46).

The passions narrative are key to the formation of each Gospel. Strange as it may seem at first sight, the suffering and death of Jesus was a major focus of the good news proclaimed by the first Christians. Of course that good news included the resurrection. But Jesus' entry into risen life held little meaning apart from his sufferings unto death. And only in the light of his passion, death and resurrection did the rest of Jesus' life come to be seen as good news.

The Lucan writer, also responsible for the Acts of the Apostles, had a very definite historical perspective. Such a perspective included an awareness of a developing faith insight into the meaning of Jesus' life, death and resurrection. This developing faith insight into the universal significance of Jesus was the necessary foundation for the beginnings of any viable Christology, one that would include Soteriology, the study of Jesus as Savior of the world.

The end of the Lucan Gospel presents a very interesting command of Jesus, one which makes room for a genuine growth in faith. Jesus enjoined his disciples to "stay in the city, until you are clothed with power from on high" (Lk 24:49). Then Luke-Acts gives us the account of Pentecost, the event which heralded the coming of the Holy Spirit, that promised gift of power.

One of the major signs of the Spirit's transforming power was the disciples' amazing change of attitude toward Jesus' sufferings. The same apostles, who previously had understood none of Jesus' explicit statements about his pending passion and death (Lk 18:34), began to proclaim the crucified Jesus as Lord and Christ (Ac 2:36). Peter, in a spirit of compassion for his fellow Israelites' ignorance, began to explain to them "what God foretold by the mouth of all the prophets, that his Christ should suffer, he thus fulfilled." (Ac 3:18). Later, having been arrested for curing a crippled man in the name of Jesus, Peter, "filled with the Holy Spirit," boldly proclaimed to the "rulers of the people and elders, ...be it known to you, all the people of Israel, that by the name of Jesus Christ of Nazareth, whom you crucified, whom God raised from the dead, by him this man is standing before you well" (Ac 4:7f.). Furthermore, as he finished his testimony, Peter made some astounding claims about Jesus. "And there is salvation in no one else, for there is no other name under heaven given among men by which we must be saved" (Ac 4:12).

On another occasion, after the apostles had been beaten for continuing to speak in the name of Jesus, Luke reports "they left the presence of the council, rejoicing that they were counted worthy to suffer dishonor for the name" (Ac 5:41). Here we see one of the early evidences of a real joy on the part of those Christians who began to share in the same kind of suffering Jesus knew as he carried out his mission of teaching and healing.

These early texts about the first Christian community in Jerusalem testify to the apostles' growing awareness of the inherent power in Jesus' sufferings. In addition, these early testimonies indicate that those same Christians were beginning to realize with joy that there was meaning and worth in their own sufferings.

The Pauline letters also give evidence of the early Christian convictions about the power and meaning of Jesus' sufferings. To the Christians at Corinth, Paul wrote, "For Christ did not send me to baptize but to preach the gospel, and not with eloquent wisdom, lest the cross of Christ be emptied of its power. For the word of the cross is folly to those who are perishing, but to us who are being saved it is the power of God" (1 Cor 1:17, 18).

In his Second Letter to the Corinthians Paul spoke of sharing in the suffering of Christ. "For as we share abundantly in Christ's sufferings, so through Christ we share abundantly in comfort too" (2 Cor 1:5). In writing to the Galatians, Paul was even more explicit about his mysterious sharing in the passion and death of Jesus. "I have been crucified with Christ; it is no longer I who live, but Christ who lives in me; and the life I now live in the flesh I live by faith in the Son of God, who loved me and gave himself for me" (Gal 2:20).

The Philippians also heard Paul insisting that he wanted to share more and more in the sufferings of Christ wherein he would know the power of the resurrection. After he reminded this community that he himself had suffered the loss of all things to gain Christ (Ph 3:8), Paul pleaded "that I may know him and the power of his resurrection, and may share his sufferings, becoming like him in his death, that if possible I may attain the resurrection from the dead" (Ph 3:10, 11).

These letters of Paul along with the early chapters of Acts witness to the developing faith insight of the early Church with respect to the power of Jesus' sufferings. Gradually those first Christians began to realize and to proclaim that all the suffering of their Lord was not in vain. Nor was their own suffering useless. Their sufferings began to be understood as a privileged way of sharing in the sufferings of Jesus.

By the time the Letter to the Colossians was written, Paul's teaching on sharing in the sufferings of Jesus was proclaimed in a most profound text. "Now I rejoice in my sufferings for your sake, and in my flesh I complete what is lacking in Christ's afflictions for the sake of his body, that is, the church..." (Col 1:24). This statement of faith follows one of the earliest theological reflections on the reconciling effects of Jesus' sufferings and will be considered more extensively later in this study. Here it is

important to emphasize that this early Christian document
speaks of the mystery of incarnation in cosmic terms which
identify Jesus as "the image of the invisible God, the first-born of
all creation" (Col 1:15). Then the letter proclaims that Jesus, in
whom the fullness of God dwells reconciled "to himself all things,
whether on earth or in heaven, making peace by the blood of his
cross" (Col 1:19). A similar theology, emphasizing the reconciling
power of the blood of Jesus is developed in the Letter to the
Ephesians. "But now in Christ Jesus you who once were far off
have been brought near in the blood of Christ" (Eph 2:13).

As this theology of reconciliation continued to develop, the
reality of human sufferings was related more and more to the
reality of human sin. Jesus' sufferings could not be accounted for
without human malice at work, whether one considered his
lifelong sufferings of opposition and rejection, or the cruel details
of his crucifixion. But as the followers of Jesus began to ponder
the meaning of incarnation, then the meaning of Jesus' sufferings
and death took on significance of cosmic proportions. Through
Jesus, not only was human suffering given meaning, but the root
causes of suffering were radically effected. Jesus became identified
as the Lamb of God who takes away the sin of the world (Jn
1:30).

2

The Mystery of Sin

Relating Suffering and Sin

Suffering has been related to sin in various ways as people have tried to cope with evil in human existence. When the question of sin is brought into the discussion about suffering, two aspects invariably associated with sin are usually included: human culpability; a God who has been offended. Considerations of human culpability tend to focus on human freedom as gift and power for shaping one's own life positively or negatively. Such personal development or deterioration is seen as part of the ongoing history of the human family. Considerations of a God offended by sin raise further questions about how God can be intimately involved with the historical development of the creatures to whom this God has given personal freedom. And questions about a suffering God usually are raised precisely in the context of sin.

But whether the question of sin is probed in relation to suffering, human and divine, or whether sin is examined somewhat in isolation, such probings lead one again into the realm of mystery, theologically speaking. As a matter of fact, there really is no intelligibility to sin if it is not approached as mystery. Most basically, sin is mystery because it involves a personal relation with God. Sin is more than moral disorder. Sin always means a change in one's relation to God.

In the previous chapter on suffering, all that was mentioned about the "more to discover" factor in mystery applies to the mystery of sin as well as to the mystery of suffering. However, in regard to the mystery of sin, there is more to discover not only with regard to the reality of sin, but also with respect to misunderstandings and confusion caused by various pastoral orientations to sin and to sinners, misrepresentations which invariably touch directly on the mystery of God.

One of the most critical areas of confusion about the relation of suffering to sin is the opinion that all suffering is a punishment sent by God for personal sins. Two well-known stories, one in the Hebrew Scriptures and another in the Christian Gospel testify to this confusion: the story of Job and the account of the cure of the man born blind (Jn 9).

When Job's wise friends began to analyze his horrible predicament in which he experienced sufferings of all kinds, they immediately concluded he had done something terribly wrong. Obviously, in their opinion, Job had sinned. A simple solution to the problem was suggested. Job needed to confess his transgressions, make amends, and consequently, God would remove all the heaven-sent punishments afflicting poor Job.

But Job could not agree with his friends' ready diagnosis of his situation. As Job continued to proclaim his innocence, the wise friends intensified their arguments even to the point of accusing Job of actual crimes.

Job's sufferings were greatly compounded by the approach of these self-righteous wise men. Nevertheless, Job steadfastly clung to the truth about himself and about his God. Personal sins were not the cause of his sufferings. Job made that point unmistakably clear and the creator God agreed.

When Jesus cured the man born blind, he met a similar mentality about personal sins obviously causing all human sufferings. Upon seeing the blind man, the disciples asked Jesus, "Rabbi, who sinned, this man or his parents, that he was born blind?" (Jn 9:2). Jesus' forthright answer resonated with the response of the creator God in the Book of Job. Jesus responded, "It was not that this man sinned, or his parents, but that the works of God might be made manifest in him" (Jn 9:3).

The ensuing dialog between the Pharisees with the cured blind man, his parents and Jesus emphatically proclaimed the innocence of both the parents and their son as far as his blindness was concerned. Furthermore, Jesus used the occasion to give needed light on the religious interpretation of human suffering as an obvious punishment for personal sins. Jesus' concluding remarks emphasized that the man's physical blindness was not a cause for guilt, whereas the willful blindness of the Pharisees was sinful (Jn 9:41).

One of the most serious problems associated with this judgmental approach of equating suffering with punishment for sin is the image of God which prevails in such an attitude. In her book, *Suffering,* theologian Dorothy Söelle discusses this mentality in the context of sadistic theologies. She delineates three aspects of such an approach. First of all, as the almighty ruler of the world, God is seen as the one who sends all suffering. Secondly, because God is never capricious and always acts justly, all sufferings are deserved by those on whom they are inflicted. Thirdly, punishment for sin is the reason explaining all suffering.[1]

In more popular language and understandings, such sadistic theological conclusions about an almighty ruler of the universe can be recast in terms of a spy-god, a divine being who constantly watches and scrutinizes the intentions and actions of human creatures in order to keep track of their offenses and punish them accordingly. Even some art forms portraying God as an all-seeing eye have been interpreted in this fashion.

I regret to say that in working with hundreds of adult Christians in theological education, repeatedly I have found a spy-god mentality to be widespread. Furthermore, most of those adult Christians have been involved in pastoral ministry of one form or another. Sadly they testify often to a spy-god mentality among the persons with whom they minister.

Pastoral Anguish

To say that suffering should not be considered automatically a punishment for personal sin is not to say there is no relation

---

[1]Dorothy Söelle, *Suffering,* tr. Everett R. Kalin (Philadelphia: Fortress Press, 1975) p. 24.

whatever between sin and suffering. Sin hurts human persons and the earth God created. Because sin causes real harm to the creatures God loves, sin is always related to sufferings, sometimes on a massive scale as in the case of war.

However, before probing more carefully into the very nature of sin, it might be helpful to consider other pastoral mis-understandings in addition to the punishing, spy-god mentality. Facing some of the pastoral anguish caused by distorted notions of sin and even worse distortions of God can be a catalyst in our pursuit of accurate theological insight in tune with the Gospel. There is so much suffering in the world caused by sin, that we need not add more because of gross misunderstanding about sin and about God on the part of countless persons who are sincerely trying to love God and to share God's love with others day after day.

One of the most tragic examples of pastoral anguish in the history of the Church is that of those mothers whose babies died before they were baptized. Usually such mothers were told their babies would not be able to enter heaven because they died in original sin. Considering the fact that until very recently, women were prevented from engaging in theological study, mothers had little choice but to accept such theological opinion as authoritative even though in their heart of hearts they had serious questions about what kind of God would prevent an innocent baby from enjoying eternal life. Consequently, many a mother has suffered not only the death of her baby, but also the mental anguish of thinking her child was deprived of God's friendship for all eternity because her baby was born with original sin and died before the sacrament of baptism could be received. And if the mother was informed of some of Augustine's teachings on this matter, she could have agonized over her child suffering the torment of the damned.

In studying the various theological opinions on this question of unbaptized babies, one finds little or no explicit reference to the agony suffered by both mother and father in such a tragic situation. One is led to wonder how the compassionate Jesus of the Gospel fits into such theological discussion. Fortunately, a certain "sense of the faithful" gradually began to prevail in the theological developments on this question, a development which emphasized a God of merciful love to whom the destiny of unbaptized babies could be entrusted.

However, this example of unbaptized babies is not the only one in which little sensitivity to human heartache has been manifest in theological deliberations regarding sin. Children also have suffered keenly because of misconceptions regarding sin and a punishing god. Small children in particular can hardly understand, much less distinguish the various and sundry delineations between venial and mortal sin. In religious education programs of the past, and sometimes even of the present, such distinctions about sin have been presented to children. How many children have been tormented with unfounded fears about hellfire, especially as they prepared for their First Communion, a time in their lives which should be one of overwhelming joy in a beginning realization of God's wondrous love for them so evident in the gift of Jesus?

For many persons sincerely trying to live a life of faith, exaggerated guilt complexes often associated with sexuality also have caused unnecessary suffering. Not only have these persons' sense of self-worth and dignity been seriously undermined, but their loving relation with God often has been severely crippled. Consequently, much of the vitality of Christian life has been weakened, thereby curtailing the needed influence of a gospel-oriented Church in a world beset with suffering.

These brief considerations of pastoral anguish caused by misconceptions about sin all point to distorted images of a god who is concerned with revengeful punishment. The eminent moral theologian, Bernard Häring, in his book, *Sin in the Secular Age,* states emphatically that we must not "fancy a revengeful God."[2] Häring also emphasizes the dire problems caused by the Church when such a god is proclaimed directly or indirectly by the severity and harshness with which Church authorities sometimes treat those who are in need of merciful understanding and help.[3]

[2]Bernard Häring, *Sin in the Secular Age* Garden City, N.Y.: Doubleday 1974) p. 75.

[3]*Ibid.,* pp. 34, 36.

Preventing more pastoral anguish caused by misconceptions regarding the reality of sin necessitates further probing into the mystery of sin. Sin is a reality. Real sin does cause suffering. Clarifying the meaning of sin continues to be an ongoing task of Christian theologians. One key orientation to such theological inquiry is that of pursuing the relation between sin and suffering, always in the light of preventing more suffering and of healing that which already exists.

The Reality of Sin

A very significant book in the seventies, written by the prominent psychiatrist, Karl Menninger, was entitled, *What Ever Became of Sin?* Menninger's reasons for writing that treatise were stated at the end of the volume. As a psychiatrist he was convinced that the root causes of the human suffering he encountered belonged to the moral and spiritual orders. No amount of scientific analysis and treatment could heal the deepest hurts of the human person. Contrary to much popular opinion of the time, Menninger insisted that religion had a vital role to play in preventing and healing human hurt. This conviction led him to write his perceptive work on the reality of sin.

In the Roman Catholic community after the Second Vatican Council, if one pondered the amazing change of practice regarding frequent reception of the Sacrament of Reconciliation or Confession, as it was usually named, one might also ask the same question about whatever became of sin. In sharp contrast to pre-Vatican II practice, rarely does one ever see a confession line is a parish church. Has sin disappeared? Just what has become of it? Have people become indifferent or hardened? Or doesn't anyone commit sin anymore? Can sin be explained away by appealing to psychological disorders as the cause of human hurt? Has psychotherapy in one form or another taken over the former role of the confessional? Has a former routine, somewhat mechanical sacramental life been challenged by a type of boycott? Or are we perhaps in a period of reaction against some of the distortions of the past which caused so much pastoral anguish?

These questions and others about the reality of sin are largely responsible for the needed probings on the part of contemporary theologians into the mystery of sin. In his insightful work, *What A Modern Catholic Believes About Sin*, theologian John Shea wrote from his pastoral experience as a priest in the archdiocese of Chicago. He noted significant shifts of emphasis emerging in the post-Vatican II Catholic community in regard to sin. Instead of viewing sin predominantly in ways that were limited to personal concerns, people were beginning to consider sin in its social ramifications. Sins of omission were being faced rather than a concentration focused almost totally on sins of commission. A legalistic mentality which viewed sin as a matter of transgressing laws was being replaced by an understanding of sin as that which hurts persons, especially the one who sins.[4]

Perhaps this shift away from a legalistic mentality is the most important development in the new pastoral orientation to sin. Clearly such a shift of emphasis is true to the Gospel wherein we find so many examples of Jesus challenging a legalistic mentality toward transgressions of the Mosaic law. Such a legalistic mentality tends to focus on keeping or breaking laws with little or no regard for human need and human suffering. Most of Jesus' sabbath cures testified to the dire need of undoing such a critical misconception of sin. Time and time again Jesus corrected such distortions of the law and of sin by insisting on the all-important law of love, of genuine care and concern for all the members of God's human family, especially the poorest and neediest ones.

In our times as a legalistic mentality regarding sin gives way to a more personal focus, a growing realization is developing regarding the importance of sins of omission. From a legalistic point of view, actions which do not break a specific law can be ignored as far as sin is concerned. It is difficult to categorize sins of omission in a legalistic way. Sins of omission concern the great law of compassionate love. As Jesus makes clear in Matthew's

[4]John Shea, *What A Modern Catholic Believes About Sin* (Chicago: The Thomas More Press, 1971) p. 10.

description of the last judgment, the focus on sin from God's point of view is on what people did or did not do for those who were hungry, thirsty and imprisoned (Mt 25:31f.).

Undoing a legalistic mentality regarding sin is also closely related to the growing awareness of sin's social ramifications. The renewed focus on the human suffering caused by sin can hardly be limited solely to those in one's immediate surroundings. If for no other reason, mass media alerts us continually to worldwide suffering. Delving into the causes of such problems as world hunger has been instrumental in creating a new vocabulary about the mystery of sin. Today's discussions about sin include the issues of social sin and of sinful structures in society and even in the Church.

Other pertinent comments regarding new understandings and emphases toward sin are found in *The Mystery of Sin and Forgiveness*, edited by the Jesuit theologian, Michael Taylor. In the Introduction, he highlights key factors which account for new perspectives on sin. In Taylor's view, the process of secularization along with technological progress have given new freedom to some persons enabling them to reflect on their human identity and consequent responsibilities to themselves and to others. Taylor claims that psychological reflection has resulted in an awareness of one's inner self along with a conviction that meaningful interpersonal relations are necessary for self-fulfillment. Taylor also points to the influence of mass communications in creating global awareness of human needs and responsibilities.[5]

Invaluable scriptural insights have contributed also to the recent theological probings into the mystery of sin. A few of the key words used to describe sin resonate well with some of the contemporary understandings of sin, provided those key words are heard in the context of God's covenantal love embracing the human family.

Interestingly enough, the images of missing the mark, ignoring the roadsign, overstepping or stumbling are all associated with

---

[5]Michael Taylor, ed., *The Mystery of Sin and Forgiveness* (Staten Island, N.Y.: Alba House, 1971) p.xii.

the vocabulary used in the Hebrew Scriptures to describe sin. Such images indicate an understanding of the covenant as a way of life, a going somewhere, along with the possibility of getting detoured or even lost.

In the prophetic literature invariably the detours and stumblings are associated with actions against one's neighbor, particularly the poor. As a result of such actions, usually in the social sphere, the persons responsible experienced a hardening of heart—another frequent expression in Hebraic writings to describe sin. Such hardness of heart meant a turning away from the God of the covenant. A loving relation between the sinner and God was sundered. Our English word, sin, carries this meaning of sundered—torn apart, broken.

Such descriptions of sin indicate that sin causes interacting repercussions involving the one who sins, other persons who are hurt by the sin, and God who is rejected in some way because of the sin. Consequently, loving personal relations are harmed whenever and wherever sin enters the picture. The person or persons responsible are on the road to self-destruction if the sinful actions persist.

Today's descriptive vocabulary for sin includes words such as alienation, divisiveness, emptiness, anxiety. Emerging from contemporary philosophical, psychological and sociological insights into the use and misuse of human freedom, such words tend to focus more sharply on the harmful effects sin causes in the life of the person who sins. Frequently, the word, sin, is identified with its devastating personal effects on the sinner, more than it is identified with a specific action.

The emphasis on personal deterioration resulting from sin can be associated readily with the disruptive power of sin at work in societal relations. In this context sin is sometimes described as a power at work in the world. As Shea points out, sin is an ever-present reality to be contended with, a constant pressure, a real force with a dynamism all its own.[6]

Perhaps no one has contributed greater insight recently into

[6]Shea, *What*, p. 81.

the power of sin at work in the world than the eminent Dutch Jesuit theologian, Piet Schoonenberg. He has carefully developed what might be called a *situation* approach to the reality of sin. Although much of his thought on the question of a sinful situation pertains to the doctrine of original sin and will be considered later in this study, some of his reflections are pertinent here.

In Schoonenberg's masterful work, *Man and Sin*, he describes the term situation, in relation to human freedom.

> All influences which pass from one free person to another free person as such, respecting the latter's freedom and appealing to it, may be lumped together under the term *situation*. My free action always puts the other into a situation, which appeals to him for good or for evil, which provides him with help or withdraws that help from him, which presents values or keeps them away from him. That situation determines his freedom not in the sense that it forces him to perform a good or evil action, but in the sense that it obliges him to react to it, for good or for evil, or to forego a reaction as the result of his own free decision.[7]

These penetrating comments on the relation of human free choices to environmental impact give needed emphasis on the societal implications of all sin. These reflections testify also to human solidarity because of the continual interaction between free choices and historical situations.

Countless examples in human history could be given to illustrate such continuous interaction. One example may suffice. The decision to tolerate slavery at the time the United States was being forged as a new nation resulted in untold human agony on slave ships, on plantations, in underground railroads, in city slums and segregated neighborhoods as racism continued generation after generation to wound and scar an entire people. No

---

[7]Piet Schoonenberg, *Man and Sin*, tr. Joseph Donceel (Notre Dame: University of Notre Dame Press, 1965) p. 104.

citizen of this country has been unaffected by the sin of racism. Quite obviously, Black people have suffered far more than others.

However, in the light of the Gospel, any person who has been or is freely and actively involved in perpetuating racism in any form is inflicting self-destruction on his or her own person in addition to inflicting suffering on those who are the victims of racist policies, attitudes and actions. The personal relations of love, necessary for genuine self-fulfillment are made impossible by the hatred underlying racism. The repercussions of such hatred may be imperceptible at times, but all the personal relations of a racist are affected because of the ongoing personal deterioration racism causes.

It is precisely in this area of human personal relations that the personal relation to God must be faced. Perhaps no New Testament writer made this point more clear than the author of 1 John who raised a radical question: "But if any one has the world's goods and sees his brother in need, yet closes his heart against him, how does God's love abide in him?" (1 Jn 3:17).

At this point in our considerations of the reality of sin, it might be helpful to recall that sin is more than moral disorder. Sin is a reality in the religious order because sin has no intelligibility if one's relation to God is not taken into account. Shea goes so far as to claim that the meaning of sin will be rediscovered only insofar as the category "before God" is reinterpreted.[8] Sin is concerned with personal relationships far more than with actions. And the personal relations in question include one's personal relation to God.

Once again we might turn to the Johannine writer who emphatically proclaimed, "God is love" (1 Jn 4:16). In three simple words this letter to the early Christians summarized the theology of Israel's first and most basic commandment. "I am the Lord your God, who brought you out of the land of Egypt, out of the house of bondage. You shall have no other gods before me" (Ex 20:2, 3). This commandment recalls God's love in action. It is the first commandment because it lays the foundation of everything else which follows for the people of the covenant.

---

[8]Shea, *What*, p. 13.

If Israel was going to live as a covenanted people, then Israel had to live in a love relationship with God. Amazingly enough, the covenant could be described as a friendship bond with the creator of heaven and earth. Moses' experience with God is described in the Book of Exodus in terms of intimate friendship. In prayerful dialog, Moses pleaded for the continued presence of Yahweh throughout the covenanted peoples' desert journey to the promised land (Ex 33:12-17). Regardless of the terrible infidelity involved in the golden calf episode (Ex 32:1f.), Moses reminded Yahweh that only the ongoing presence of their God would witness to Israel's covenantal favor. And Yahweh replied to Moses, "This request, too, which you have just made, I will carry out, because you have found favor with me and you are my intimate friend" (Ex 33:17).[9]

Friendship, including the friendship bond of covenant with God, always means sharing life together. One main reason my friends are my friends is that we enjoy one another's company. We like to be with each other, to talk things over, to do things together. Understanding the covenant relation in the context of a friendship bond with God means all that human friendship can mean and more. Both partners in this covenant relation want to be present to each other. Again it might be helpful to recall how frequently in Israel's history Yahweh promised to be with the covenanted people. In this context, how significant are Jesus' final words in the Gospel of Matthew. ". . . I am with you always, to the close of the age" (Mt 28:20).

Covenant partners want to talk things over as friends, as we know from the experience of Moses and the other great spiritual leaders in Israel's history. Such loving listening and responding is one way to consider prayer. In fact, listening to God is a most basic way of describing prayer in the Hebrew Scriptures. The third Isaian servant song is a key text in this regard. "Morning by morning he wakens, he wakens my ear to hear as those who are taught. The Lord God has opened my ear . . . " (Is 50:4, 5).

---

[9]Here the *New American Bible* translation is used because of the way friendship is mentioned explicitly.

Covenant partners will also share life by doing things together. Mutual concern for all of God's creatures will prompt the actions of those who are truly God's friends. The reluctant prophet Jonah matured in his friendship with God as he learned about God's care of the animals along with human creatures. In offsetting Jonah's desire for the destruction of the wicked city Nineveh, God reminded him of the little children who couldn't tell right from left, and also of the animals who would suffer. God concluded a conversation with Jonah by asking, "And should not I pity Nineveh, that great city, in which there are more than a hundred and twenty thousand persons who do not know their right hand from their left, and also much cattle?" (Jon 4:11).

Most basically, the covenant of friendship with God means a mutual personal relationship of genuine love. Consequently, God must be remembered and considered as the loving God whose fidelity is unquestioned. Only then, can a human response of love toward God be possible. No wonder the commandment given to Moses is so crystal clear and direct. "You shall have no other gods before me" (Ex 20:3). False gods of whatever sort, punishing gods and spy gods included, cannot evoke an authentic response of love on the part of a human person. When this most basic relation of love of God is upset or distorted in any way, the human person begins to suffer a disorientation which effects all other relationships. God offered the covenant before the decalogue, the ten commandments, were proposed. That decalogue could only be understood, much less lived, in the context of the covenant.

Perhaps the Hebraic concept of *shalom* speaks to this covenant relation in a most positive way. When used as a greeting, *shalom* is a prayerful wish for human wholeness and harmony with all of creation. In the New Testament, the special gift of Jesus' own peace is referred to as *shalom*. Such wholeness and harmony depends first and foremost on one's loving relation to God. This loving relation to God is expressed most frequently through one's loving and caring relation to others.

However, it is one's loving relation to God which is most basic for the harmonious, right-ordered love of oneself. Nothing can give a person a greater sense of self-worth and dignity, of *shalom*, than the realization that one is truly loved by God. To be loved by

God means one is truly good and loveable. Without such a realization of one's own goodness, a person is prone to compensate in many ways, often at the expense of other's well being. As a result, real harm can be caused to others and to oneself; sin can be committed.

The ordering of the ten commandments is not a haphazard arrangement. Nor is it an over-simplification to say that the way the first commandment is kept determines how the other commandments will be taken care of. How significant that the Deuteronomic writer singles out the first commandment and recasts it in terms of wholehearted love. "Hear, O Israel: The Lord our God is one Lord; and you shall love the Lord your God with all your heart, and with all your soul, and with all your might" (Dt 6:4, 5).

When Jesus was asked about which law was greatest, he not only referred to this Deuteronomic statement, but immediately he added the commandment to love one's neighbor as oneself. Jesus answered, "The first is, 'Hear O Israel: The Lord our God, the Lord is one; and you shall love the Lord with all your soul, and with all your mind, and with all your strength.' The second is this, "You shall love your neighbor as yourself.' There is no other commandment greater than these" (Mk 12:29-31). In the Matthean version of this episode, Jesus emphasized the foundational character of this way of love in his concluding remark. "On these two commandments depend all the law and the prophets" (Mt 22:40).

In the eucharistic discourse of the Johannine Gospel, Jesus identified the knowing of God with eternal life. "And this is eternal life, that they know thee the only true God, and Jesus Christ whom thou hast sent" (Jn 17:3). The same eucharistic discourse portrays Jesus as the one who shows us what God is really like. When Philip requested Jesus to show the apostles the Father, Jesus replied, "He who has seen me has seen the Father" (Jn 14:8f.).

For Christians it can hardly be over-emphasized that Jesus is the way to see who God is and how God acts. The God of Jesus is the same covenant God of the Hebrew Scriptures. The God of Jesus is a God of unbelievable compassion, a God who wants to share life with all human persons. The God of Jesus is not a harsh, revengeful, punishing deity.

However, in making such a claim for the God of Jesus, one cannot ignore the many scriptural texts which portray God in some punishing fashion. Such portrayals can be found throughout the Bible, from the dire threats of the prophets to Matthew's account of the last judgment. Sometimes it even seems as though refusal to live in a covenantal relationship would result in the infliction of punishments by an angry, rejected deity. The same Deuteronomic section which includes the convenantal command to love God with all one's heart and soul and might, also includes a description of an angry God. "You shall not go after other gods, of the gods of the peoples who are round about you; for the Lord your God in the midst of you is a jealous God; lest the anger of the Lord your God be kindled against you, and he destroy you from off the face of the earth" (Dt 6:14, 15). In all honesty, isn't it somewhat difficult to grow in a genuine friendship with someone, including God, if that person threatens punishment?

The issue of punishment raises additional questions about the justice of God. Are not the good to be rewarded and the wicked to be punished, as Matthew's last judgment account indicates? Doesn't the God of Jesus play fair with the human family?

Some of these pertinent questions about the image of a punishing god are treated more extensively in other sections of this study. At this juncture, the question of an angry, punishing god image must be faced in relation to the reality of sin. Some may argue that fear of punishment prevents sin. There is certainly more than a grain of truth in that position. But today's insights into the reality of sin and its root causes call into question the whole issue of punishing deities and the prevention of sin.

Fear of punishment as a moral deterrent is being understood more and more as a sign of personal immaturity. In his well-known study, *The Philosophy of Moral Development*, Lawrence Kohlberg identifies this mentality as belonging to the earliest stage of moral development.[10] Fear of punishment is hardly the

---

[10]Lawrence Kohlberg, *The Philosophy of Moral Development*, Vol. 1 (New York: Harper & Row, 1981) p. 409.

kind of motivation which calls forth the human responses characteristic of personal maturity, of one who is truly blessed with the
wholeness and harmony of *shalom*

In regard to the scriptural texts themselves, whether they are
found in the Hebrew or Christian Scriptures, those texts implying
some sort of revengeful punishment on the part of God must be
understood in the context of a gradual developing faith insight on
the part of the covenanted community. Not only individual
persons mature in faith, but communities also are called to a
developing life of faith. False notions and images of God need to
be replaced by ever more accurate perceptions of God. In the
Hebrew Scriptures, later texts such as Second Isaiah and the
Song of Songs give clear evidence of Israel's maturing faith life.
Those texts proclaim God's wondrous love in powerful and
beautiful ways.

Right from the beginning, the creator God of the covenant was
the God of compassionate love. However, in the earliest stages of
Israel's history, this covenanted people tended to interpret God's
actions in ways that reflected their own immature human reactions. Gradually from experience they learned God's ways were
not theirs. To that effect, what a significant proclamation is found
in the final chapter of Second Isaiah.

> For my thoughts are not your thoughts,
> neither are your ways my ways, says the Lord.
> For as the heavens are higher than the earth,
> so are my ways higher than your ways
> and my thoughts than your thoughts

(Is 55:8, 9).

In considering the many problems connected with a distorted
image of a punishing God, and the damaging effects of such an
image on a human person, one needs to understand how punishment is understood theologically, rather than juridically. In the
juridic order, punishment of some sort follows a crime. Juridically
speaking, punishment is some kind of penalty levied against a
person who has been found guilty of breaking a civil law. This
pattern does not apply in the theological order. There punishment

is seen as intrinsic to sin. That is to say, sin carries within itself a destructive power. As Schoonenberg explains, sin remains in its punishment.[11] Consequently, God should never be imaged as inflicting some extra penalty when sin is committed. Rather, God is concerned about preventing sin and its ongoing effects because of all the suffering that sin inflicts on the creatures God loves. Scriptural texts relating punishment to an angry God are often misinterpreted according to the juridical practice of inflicting punishment following a crime. To correct the many harmful misinterpretations of God's role in relation to sin's punishment, one must invoke the theological understanding of punishment being intrinsic to sin.

Perhaps two scenes in the life of Jesus will highlight this distinction between the juridical and theological orders. There are two Lucan accounts describing Jesus lamenting over his beloved city, Jerusalem. These episodes provide two of the most touching stories in the Lucan Gospel.

The first episode is situated in the midst of the growing opposition Jesus met as he fulfilled his prophetic mission. After Jesus was warned that Herod wanted to kill him, he cried out,

> O Jerusalem, Jerusalem, killing the prophets
> and stoning those who are sent to you! How
> often would I have gathered your children
> together as a hen gathers her brood under
> her wings, and you would not! Behold,
> your house is forsaken. And I tell you,
> you will not see me until you say,
> 'Blessed is he who comes in the name of
> the Lord!' "

(Luke 13:34, 35).

The second episode takes place as Jesus approached Jerusalem at the time of his passion and death. Luke presents a very human Jesus agonizing over the pending destruction of the holy city.

---

[11]Schoonenberg, *Man*, p. 63.

> And when he drew near and saw the city
> he wept over it, saying, "Would that
> even today you knew the things that
> make for peace! But now they are hid
> from your eyes. For the days shall
> come upon you, when your enemies will
> cast up a bank about you and surround
> you, and hem you in on every side, and
> dash you to the ground, you and your
> children within you, and they will not
> leave one stone upon another in you;
> because you did not know the time of
> your visitation."
>
> (Lk 19:41-44).

In these two episodes two key points are illustrated regarding the image of God. First of all, God does not inflict suffering as a punishment. Secondly, sin carries its own punishment. Regarding the image of God presented in these episodes, we must ponder Jesus agonizing over Jerusalem to the point of weeping. He used an image of most tender compassion to try to describe his feelings—that of a mother hen attempting to gather her fragile little chicks under her wings. In reflecting on such imagery, along with the picture of Jesus truly weeping, we must remember who Jesus is if we are going to comprehend something about God's attitude and actions in such circumstances. We also must realize a free human choice was responsible for the tragic circumstances. To be more precise, many human choices of an entire people were responsible for the devastating events predicted by Jesus. Referring to Jerusalem's response of rejection to God's covenantal invitation, Jesus simply stated, "and you would not."

Both texts make it clear that the rejection of God's love in Jesus causes severe problems. A blindness results regarding God's visitation. Genuine peace or *shalom* becomes impossible to experience. Jerusalem's house becomes forsaken; her buildings totally destroyed; her inhabitants, even her children, cruelly murdered. The sin of rejection lets loose a terribly destructive power. For this reason, Jesus wept.

Perhaps in the light of these considerations of God's reactions to sin, we can see somewhat more clearly why the reality of sin is mystery. Sin in some way is always a rejection of love and therefore is somehow a rejection of God who is love. The more deliberate the rejection, the greater the disorientation in a person's life and in a community's life. We are created to enjoy God's life of love. When that basic orientation is skewed or disrupted, our whole being suffers the repercussions. All our societal relations suffer as well.

This focus on God's loving invitation to friendship, to dialog, to sharing life, has been one of the recent key orientations to a most difficult aspect of the mystery of sin, namely, its origins. At this point in our study of the reality of sin, a brief consideration of the problems and probings connected with the doctrine of original sin is in order. Such a consideration can be very instrumental in undoing the widespread misconceptions regarding a wise, just and loving God, one who really invites us to friendship in time and in eternity. In addition, some former theories of original sin have caused horrible misconceptions regarding the goodness and potential in human persons made in the image and likeness of God.

The Origin of Sin

Recently a colleague shared with me a brief discussion which occurred with a student after class. The class itself had nothing to do directly with theology. In all sincerity this student wanted to know how we could ever consider God to be good and just when women were punished more severely than men because of original sin. This student's question stated quite boldly some of the terrible distortions about God and about the human family, particularly women, that abound because of confusion over the meaning of original sin. Today's feminist theologians continually point out the grave injustices inflicted on women because of erroneous interpretations of the Genesis story. In addition, both women and men often suffer from a sense of inferiority and continual guilt because of the ways they have been taught about their human sinfulness. Often, actions for justice and for peace have been stymied because theories of original sin have perpetuated a sense of futility about changing unjust structures and patterns of human conduct such as war. And then there is the history of pastoral anguish referred to earlier regarding the fate of unbaptized babies. In the face of all this negativity and confusion, a Christian readily might wonder just who really is redeemed by Jesus and just what that redemption really means.

In their efforts to give some intelligibility to the mystery of sin's origin in human life, theologians invariably have associated their teaching on the origin of sin with the undoing of the power of sin by Jesus. As a matter of fact, there is really no intelligibility to a doctrine of original sin if that mystery is not seen in the light of Jesus' redeeming action. But the question of Jesus' redeeming action has to confront the fact of ongoing human sin and suffering as well as the question of sin's beginnings.

Some of the more recent theological insights into the reality of sin also pertain to the origin of sin. The emphases on personal relations and on societal repercussions have given needed clarity on the many questions surrounding sin's beginnings in human history. It is hoped such theological clarifications will relieve and heal some of the pastoral anguish already caused by grievous misunderstandings of the doctrine of original sin and prevent such suffering in the future.

One of the most recent studies on the mystery of sin is *Community and Disunity: Symbols of Grace and Sin,* by Benedictine abbot, Jerome Theisen. In chapter 1, entitled, "Sin: Attempts to Explain its Origin," Theisen not only presents historical attempts to explain sin's beginnings, but he also summarizes several key contemporary theories regarding original sin.

Of those recent theories, one in particular has proved quite helpful in throwing some light on the mystery of sin's origins. I refer to the painstaking work of two Jesuit theologians, Maurizio Flick and Zolton Alzeghy. Their writings began to appear in the sixties and have had considerable influence ever since.

Focusing on the wondrous destiny of human persons to live a life of genuine friendship with God, these theologians highlight the issue of human development by way of loving personal relations, especially with God. They suggest that at the very beginning of the human evolutionary process, an initial refusal to enter into a loving dialogical relation with God resulted in a situation of dialogical alienation, one which greatly hinders personal growth, even to the point of making personal fulfillment impossible. The repercussions of such dialogical alienation are cumulative, resulting in a world which constantly curtails, if not totally prevents the possibility of loving response to God. As a result of this rejection of God's invitation to friendship, the possibilities of loving human relations are seriously hampered.

This particular explanation of sin's origins resonates with much of the current thinking on the meaning of sin with its emphasis on personal relationships and on problematic situations everywhere in the world. Focusing on the beginnings of dialogical alienation is one way to understand the Genesis writer who wrestled with the mysterious origin of sin in God's created universe, a universe originally proclaimed by God as good.

Misinterpretations of the Genesis story have been widespread for a long time and have worked havoc in Christian life. Fortunately the writings of eminent scripture scholars, including Dubarle, Gelin, and Lyonnet, have been very instrumental in correcting some of the misleading errors of interpretation regarding the Book of Genesis.

One of the first principles to be aware of in understanding a writing like Genesis is that the authors of such works are attempting to give some intelligibility to the origin of the world as they know it in the light of their own experience. For some people it is very confusing to call the Genesis story of creation a myth, if by myth one means some kind of make-believe fairy tale. The Genesis myth is dealing with reality, but not in the sense of precise historical data as we think of it today. Myth, as we find it in Genesis, is a way of expressing the human condition by way of story. We must remember no one documented the beginnings of the human race with TV cameras and tape recorders.

Most Christians are accustomed to the terminology of "the fall" as a way of describing the third chapter of Genesis. Today that terminology is questioned because of the way it aggravates the negative connotations about human dignity so often associated with explanationsof original sin. In any event, it is basic to the theology of Genesis that all of God's creation is genuinely good as the first chapter insists. Furthermore, the first eleven chapters must be included if one is to do justice to the question of sin's beginnings according to Genesis.

Often the origin of sin is described as a first free act of disobedience at the very beginning of the human race. Such disobedience is a way of saying what God wants is rejected. If the Genesis story is seen in the light of God's offer of covenantal friendship, perhaps one can understand how that story contains the elements inherent in any sin.

From the covenant experience in history, Christians have come to realize their destiny is that of enjoying friendship with God in time and in eternity. Such friendship can be initiated only by God. Such friendship must be freely accepted by those created and called to be God's friends. Such enjoyment of God's friendship includes the enjoyment of God's friends also.

The symbolism in the Genesis story speaks of the mystery of human friendship with God. Walking and talking with God in a beautiful garden is one way to say that God and human persons made in God's image and likeness were enjoying life together.

In regard to the so-called "forbidden fruit," scripture scholars tend to agree that the symbolism here is a matter of human beings attempting to go beyond their creaturely status in some way. However, in the perspective of God's invitation to friendship, a relationship which in many respects goes far beyond creature-hood, I wonder if the disobedience involved was more in the order of refusing the trust and risk-taking which all friendship demands.

The Genesis writer is most realistic about the effects of such a rejection of God's plan. Not only is the relation between God and human beings radically altered, but the personal relation between man and woman began to shift drastically. Human family relations experienced deterioration and enmity as the Cain and Abel story illustrates. The harmony of the entire created universe was upset, typified by the story of the flood. Life was in jeopardy, in its beginnings and in its possibilities for continued sustenance and development. Death stalked the earth as human conflicts multiplied "and the earth was filled with violence" (Gn 6:11).

The Genesis story of sin's disastrous effects culminates with the Tower of Babel story in chapter 11. Using the image of a Babylonian ziggurat with its architectural design of stair-steps to the realm of the gods, in ingenious fashion the Genesis writer portrays a drastically divided human community. In contemporary terms, the Babel story is a picture of dialogical alienation at its worst.

To appreciate the profound theology of the Babel account, one must relate the episode to the story describing the beginnings of the human race. Here again, the question of friendship with God comes to the fore as a basic foundation for both stories. In the attempt to build the Tower of Babel, the human community is pictured as trying to find a way to achieve greatness by reaching the heavenly realm solely through their own efforts. Whatever else such a vain attempt means, it certainly is not the way of friendship. Arrogance and pursuit of power and prestige have replaced the trust and love necessary for friendship. Dialog with God is totally absent. There is no human response to God because there is no listening to God. The tragic consequences result in the lack of genuine dialog in the human community also. Divisiveness and fragmentation follow inevitably for the entire human race.

The presentation of sin's cumulative disastrous effects as depicted in the early chapters of Genesis is a helpful background for understanding recent insights into the "sin of the world." Such a phrase is descriptive of all the accumulated sin down through the centuries. Schoonenberg's theology of the sin situation is another way to consider the sin of the world. This insidious history of sin did have a beginning. But more than the first sin is responsible for the situation of sin which has contaminated the goodness of a loving God's creation. The world as we know it is not the world God intended.

Every human being is born into a world disfigured by sin. Unfortunately, some explanations of original sin tended to give the impression that the very act of human generation was sinful. Such an erroneous opinion has compounded the negative and suspicious attitudes toward the goodness and giftedness of human sexuality. The sharing of life and the giving of new life are meant to be beautiful human expressions of God's creative love. The difficulty lies not in the coming-to-be of a new person, but in a certain resistance to growth in love which every person meets. This resistance to love, particularly to the love of God, is intrinsic to the cumulative sin of the world and has mysteriously found its way into the human heart.

Since the sixteenth century various explanations of original sin usually depend in some way on the teachings of the Council of Trent. That Council's formulations of the doctrine of original sin did not determine "the causal connection between procreation and original sin," as Schoonenberg points out.[12] To make a case for some such connection goes beyond the teaching of Trent. Furthermore, conciliar teaching always must be understood in its own historical frame of reference. What Trent did affirm was the unity of the human race and our solidarity in Jesus who saves us all from sin. Present day theological considerations of the universality of a sin situation give needed clarification to the teachings of Trent and provide corrective insights regarding the many misunderstandings of the Church's official teachings on the origin of sin.

As this doctrinal teaching develops, one can hope that the work of today's theologians will be fruitful in highlighting the great goodness of our creator God in whose image we are made. As such theological work continues, sin in all of its ramifications will be seen for what it is most basically—a refusal to accept God's invitation to convenantal friendship. But even more importantly, needed clarity about the mystery of sin will provide even greater insight into the mystery of Jesus whom God sent because of love for the world (Jn 3:16).

---

[12]*Ibid.*, p. 174.

3

The Mystery of Jesus

Jesus Enters a World Burdened with Suffering and Sin

Several aspects of Jesus' approach to suffering and sin have been treated already in the previous two chapters. Particularly in chapter 1, "The Mystery of Suffering," the focus was on the Lucan writings. Now as we try to see more penetratingly into the mystery of Jesus, one more Lucan passage may serve as a helpful introduction.

The Lucan Canticle, commonly known in the Christian tradition as the *Benedictus*, with great artistry proclaims Jesus' entry into the world. This early hymn, most likely incorporated into the Gospel from the early Jewish-Christian liturgies, uses the image of a rising sun with all of its life-giving power to describe the coming of Jesus (Lk 1:78, 79).

The entire *Benedictus* (Lk 1:68-79) presents a rather profound theology of the mission of Jesus. Exulting over the birth of John the Baptist who would prepare the way for Jesus, Zechariah, the father of John, proclaims the wonders of Israel's God. The Canticle begins with a prayer of praise. "Blessed be the Lord God of Israel, for he has visited and redeemed his people." Then, referring to God's great fidelity in fulfilling the promises made through the "holy prophets from of old," Zechariah describes briefly the difficult life situation into which Jesus would come as the "dawn from on high." How starkly this Canticle describes the predicament of the covenanted people. They were sitting "in darkness and in the shadow of death" (Lk 1:79).

In remembering the holy covenant made to Abraham, God was now going to save the people from their enemies, from the hand of all who hated them (Lk 1:71). Consequently, the covenanted people could serve without fear (Lk 1:74). All the days of their lives they would be able to live in holiness and righteousness before God (Lk 1:75). Furthermore, in his preparatory role as prophet of the Most High, John the Baptist would give knowledge of salvation to God's people in the forgiveness of their sins (Lk 1:77). All this was happening "through the tender mercy of our God" (Lk 1:78).

To grasp some of the theological understandings incorporated into this brief and beautiful song, one must be aware of the covenant implications sounded therein. In typical Lucan fashion with its characteristic outlook on the entire human family, the covenant is related to Abraham explicitly, rather than to Moses. In our comments on the theology of Genesis regarding the origin of sin and its cumulative, devastating effects, we went as far as the Tower of Babel story in chapter 11. The Abraham story begins in chapter 12.

There once again, God gives an offer of friendship, an invitation to go with God into a whole new life situation. Abram, as he was then known, responded in obedient trust and "went, as the Lord had told him" (Gn 12:4). God and Abram started on a life journey of faithful friendship, of covenantal trust and love.

When Zechariah's Canticle proclaims the Abrahamic covenant, it does so in the light of Israel's history. All through the centuries God's fidelity was experienced without question; not so with Israel. Sin had entered into the lives of God's people. Forgiveness was needed. Broken personal relations had to be restored. Fear needed to be replaced by love. Only the tender mercy of God could accomplish this salvation. Now God was visiting Israel once again in the person of Jesus who would guide the people "into the way of peace," of genuine *shalom*.

One of the most significant recent studies of Jesus is entitled *Jesus the Compassion of God*, written by the widely known theologian, Monika Hellwig. Many insights from this remarkable Christology influence this present study. Reflecting on this new title for Jesus, I would like to suggest that Zechariah's Canticle readily could be subtitled, "A Song to Jesus, the Compassion of God." All the tender mercy of Israel's God proclaimed in this song is promised to culminate in Jesus.

Tender mercy is one way to speak of compassion. Compassion refers to a being-with-another-in-whatever-happens. Mercy is love poured out for those in special need. Often mercy implies forgiveness. Mercy and compassion continually interact with each other, especially when what-happens-to-another causes suffering.

In the *Benedictus* the mystery of Jesus' incarnation is presented in terms of Israel's compassionate God of covenantal friendship. This is the God who loves so passionately as to personally enter in the human situation burdened with suffering and sin. In Johannine terms this is the God whose love for the world prompted the sending of Jesus, the Lamb of God, to take away the world's sin.

Jesus Lives and Dies in Trust

If the very essence of sin can be described as a rejection of God who is love, then Jesus began to meet sin from the beginning of his life as described in the infancy narratives of both Luke and Matthew. Luke tells us "there was no place for them in the inn" (Lk 2:7). Matthew gives the tragic account of Herod's cruel, insidious attempt to destroy Jesus (Mt. 2:1f.). Theologically speaking these infancy narratives are previews of what is to follow in the adult life of Jesus.

Throughout his life Jesus suffered keenly from the sin of rejection. According to the Lucan Gospel, the Nazareth synagogue episode at the beginning of his public life concludes with the infuriated crowd trying to hurl Jesus over a cliff (Lk 4:28-30). We have mentioned already the continual problems Jesus faced when he manifested his compassion by curing people on the sabbath. The Johannine Gospel presents the almost constant argumentation Jesus faced with some of the religious leaders (e.g. Jn 5:16-47; 7:32f.; 8:12f.). Mark tells us even some of Jesus' own family members and friends misunderstood him (Mk 3:19-21).

Jesus' reaction to all this opposition is a most important aspect of his life. Perhaps no contemporary theologian has focused more poignantly on Jesus' own faith and trust in the face of such suffering than the Salvadorean Jesuit, Jon Sobrino. His liberation Christology entitled in English, *Christology at the Crossroads*, may be considered a genuine breakthrough with respect to understanding Jesus' developing life of faith. Chapter 4 is entitled "The Faith of Jesus: Its Relevance for Christology and Following Jesus."

Sobrino uses what might be termed a following-of-Jesus approach in order to highlight the way Jesus' own faith really grew stronger and actually developed throughout his life and in the mystery of his death. After Jesus met with increasing antagonism and resistance in Galilee, his faith in his God underwent a profound change which Sobrino describes as a "trust against trust."[1] The passion predictions are inserted in each synoptic Gospel at this critical time in Jesus' ministry (Mk 8:31; Mt 16: 21-28; Lk 9:22-27).

One way to grasp the significance of this radical shift in Jesus' pattern of action is to ponder the Isaian servant songs. There too, a radical change in the servant's life is indicated in the third song (Is 50: 4-9). The first two songs picture a person actively involved in bringing good news to the poor, sight to the blind, release to captives (Is 42:1-7; 49:1-6). But in the third song a vastly different motif is introduced. After highlighting the servant's prayerful intimacy with God, the song sounds the note of violent opposition to the servant's mission. The servant entered a new phase of life—the path of suffering in love.

After the crisis in Galilee, Jesus began to experience in new ways the power of love in the midst of suffering. He began to realize that fidelity to the way of God would bring mounting opposition on the part of those who were caught in the sin of rejecting God's offer of friendship and all that meant as a way of life. The words of Isaiah's third servant song must have resonated in Jesus' mind and heart as he faced increasing resistance and

---

[1]Jon Sobrino, *Christology at the Crossroads,* tr. John Drury (Maryknoll: Orbis, 1978) p. 94.

calculated violence. "Behold, the Lord God helps me" (Is 50:9).

In Sobrino's careful presentation of Jesus' maturing faith, often the virtues of trust and hope are so intrinsically related to faith that it is difficult to distinguish one from the other. In this present study with its focus on friendship, the virtue of trust will be emphasized as an integral aspect of faith.

A consideration of the gospel episodes depicting scenes in which Jesus met rejection, brings one to the question of Jesus' unwavering faith and trust in his God, his *Abba*. There is no other way to explain why Jesus continued in his mission with such confidence and courage. Whether Jesus faced the rejection of the crowds as in the Nazareth synagogue, or opposition by the religious leaders contending with him over his sabbath cures, never did Jesus deviate from his way of manifesting God's compassionate love for those in need.

Each of the Gospels, particularly Luke, reminds us of times in which Jesus withdrew from the pressing crowds in order to pray. Clearly Jesus needed time alone with his God. In the face of mounting hostility, there was no other way that Jesus could have continued to teach and heal those who were suffering. Jesus needed the strengthening power of prayer. In this prayer he deepened his conviction that his *Abba* could be trusted. Through prayer Jesus saw ever more clearly that God's way of entering into situations of suffering and sin was the only way which would make a difference.

Jesus's growth in faith and trust was not without struggle, as the Gospels make clear. The synoptic accounts of Jesus' temptations in the desert testify to the clash of value systems confronting Jesus as he began and continued his mission (Mt. 4:1-11; Mk 1:12-13; Lk 4:1-13). God's ways of compassionate love were not the ways of material aggrandizement and dominating power, attractive and compelling as they might appear. More than once, according to the Lucan account, Jesus had to choose the way of trust in the wise, but very different value system of his God.

As Jesus faced more and more human suffering, he saw more deeply into its root causes—sins of human selfishness at odds with the ways of God's outpouring love. Jesus not only witnessed to a different way of life, but also taught his followers ways and means to counteract and heal the ravages of sin in human life. The heart of those teachings are found in Matthew's Sermon on the Mount (Mt 5-7), paralleled by Luke's Discourse on the Plain (Lk 6:17-49).

In those discourses, especially in the beatitudes, do we find a way of human life truly in accord with the ways of a compassionate, covenantal God. The poor, gentle, the sorrowing, the merciful, those hungering and thirsting for justice, the pure in heart, the peacemakers, the persecuted—those may be called blessed because they are living God's way of love. And perhaps most surprising of all, this way of love must extend to those who, for whatever reasons, are considered enemies. They must be forgiven and treated in compassionate, loving ways.

However, this beatitude way of life did not bring immediate results. Hungering and thirsting for justice didn't automatically establish the kind of human relations which satisified the demands of justice. Forgiving enemies did not necessarily cause a change of heart and resolve a conflict, at least not right away. As Jesus continued to witness and teach this beatitude way of life, he met more and more opposition and rejection. In the face of little or no apparent success, Jesus had to learn a kind of trust in his God that apparently had little or nothing to stand on as far as results were concerned. Jesus' trust against trust can be described as a new kind of faith in his God. Sobrino goes so far as to say Jesus' conception of God changed in this process of growing in trust.[2]

As Jesus grew in a trust which enabled him confidently to leave the results of his efforts to God's providential design, a conviction deepened regarding the truth and goodness inherent in Jesus' actions. Perhaps no gospel account illustrates this conviction more strongly than the dialog with Jesus' disciples following the multiplication of the loaves as recorded in the sixth chapter of John (Jn 6:1-71, esp. 60-71). How skillfully the Johannine writer weaves together the scenes of Jesus feeding the multitude; walking on water; discoursing on the necessity of faith in himself; and promising the special gift of himself in the eucharist. Disputes and argumentation followed. "After this many of his disciples drew

[2]*Ibid.*

back and no longer went about with him" (Jn 6:66). Then Jesus asked his chosen twelve if they would leave him also.

The sixth chapter of John is remarkable on many counts. One of the most amazing aspects is Jesus' willingness to let all his followers leave him rather than compromise his own truth. Here, as in his passion, Jesus witnesses to an undaunted conviction about the rightness of his way of life and teachings. He knew his unique witness to the love of his God would be compromised if he gave in to popular opinion and acted in other ways. If people were going to see something of their covenantal God's outpouring of love regardless of their history of faithlessness, then Jesus had to witness to that love with uncompromising fidelity. He risked misunderstanding and failure. He simply had to entrust himself and all his efforts to God.

The Johannine Gospel's last supper account differs considerably from those of the synoptics. John's description of the last supper begins with Jesus washing the feet of his disciples (Jn 13:3f.). That scene as well as the entire passion is introduced with the statement, ". . . when Jesus knew that his hour had come to depart out of this world to the Father, having loved his own who were in the world, he loved them to the end" (Jn 13:1).

In the eucharistic discourse which follows, Jesus spoke of friendship as a way to describe the intimate sharing of life he had come to restore. In this context of friendship, Jesus used the image of vine and branches to highlight the mutual sharing of life which genuine friendship entails (Jn 15:1f.). He promised to those who would abide in him a fullness of joy (Jn 15:11). Then he gave his great commandment of love. "This is my commandment, that you love one another as I have loved you" (Jn 15:12).

Other characteristics of mature friendship were then given. A person must be willing to lay down one's life for one's friends. In the light of his approaching passion and death, Jesus simply stated there was no greater love than to lay down one's life (Jn 15:13).

Then Jesus proceeded to explain why he called his disciples friends rather than slaves, although he had just performed the menial task of a slave by washing the feet of his disciples. Jesus called his disciples friends because "all that I have heard from my

Father I have made known to you" (Jn 15:15). The mutual sharing of mind and heart that is described in this passage depends on the kind of trust that genuine friendship demands and enjoys. Not only was Jesus referring to the trust his disciples needed to place in him, but most surprising of all, Jesus was pledging his own trust in his disciples whom he called friends.

It was precisely this mutual trust that made possible a genuine sharing in the love of God which Jesus experienced throughout his life. Before Jesus spoke explicitly of friendship with his disciples, he referred to his own experience of God's love as the source of his love for his followers. "As the Father has loved me, so have I loved you; abide in my love" (Jn 15:9). But at that point in his life, Jesus still had to experience an undaunted trust in his God when the loving care of that God seemed totally absent.

The closer Jesus came to his death, the more he experienced an abandonment of his former hopes and dreams for the imminent coming of the reign of God's love. In some mysterious way, Jesus even experienced an abandonment by his God, his *Abba*. Through this experience of abandonment, Jesus entered most profoundly into the mystery of suffering and sin. He entered into the crux of the suffering caused by sin. On the cross he experienced his own apparent rejection *by* God as he suffered in his own person humankind's sinful rejection *of* God. It is on Calvary above all that Jesus trusted against trust.

Of all the unbelieveable anguish Jesus suffered, probably nothing could come close to his experience of abandonment by the God whom he knew and loved in a uniquely intimate way. Why did this happen? To paraphrase the question in the context of the Lucan Emmaus account, Was it really necessary that the Christ should suffer these things? (cf. Lk 24:26).

In the mystery of Jesus' death on the cross, we can see something of the lengths God will go to restore the friendship God longs to share with the human family. The rejection of Jesus by all those responsible for his death can be considered the climactic rejection of God's offer of friendship, the ultimate in human sin.[3] The crucified Jesus is God's response to this rejection.

---

[3] Cf. Piet Schoonenberg, *Man and Sin*, tr. Joseph Donceel (Notre Dame: University of Notre Dame Press, 1965) p. 110.

Jesus crucified on Calvary is the witness *par excellence* that God does not retaliate through vengeful punishment of some sort. In Jesus, God suffers the rejection caused by sin and enters into sin's consequent abandonment of God. Into this abandonment God brings the transforming power of love. In the crucified Jesus, the power of trust against trust undoes the refusal to trust which is inherent in every sin. Sin's ruptured friendship with God is done away with forever on Calvary. The possibility of the entire human family entering into friendship with God is restored. The crucified Jesus destroys forever the power of sin at its roots and gives new meaning and power to human suffering.

Attempts to Appreciate Jesus' Love for the World

On the first Good Friday the earliest followers of Jesus experienced the crucifixion of the one they thought was the promised Messiah. On that tragic day they hardly could have grasped anything of the significance of his cruel death. It was obvious that Jesus of Nazareth had suffered a criminal's death at the hands of the Roman authorities. What that death meant was not quite so obvious.

The gospel accounts of the risen Jesus are filled with mystery. Those who experienced his presence gradually moved from fear and doubt to courage and faith. Only through the action of Jesus' promised Holy Spirit did the first Christians begin to realize what Jesus' death and resurrection meant for the entire human family.

The preaching of the early Church as we know it from Peter's sermons in Acts testifies to a profound faith in the power of Jesus' death and resurrection (Ac 2:14-36; 3:12-26; 4:8-12; 10:34-43). Peter's Pentecost proclamation skillfully interweaves the prophet Joel's prediction about the coming day of the Lord; Psalm 16 with its wondrous theme of God's life-giving presence overcoming the corruption of death; Psalm 110 with its promise of Davidic exaltation; and the mystery of "this Jesus whom you crucified" whom "God has made both Lord and Christ" (Ac 2:36). Then in response to a question, Peter urged his hearers who had gathered in Jerusalem "from every nation under heaven" (Ac 2:5) to "Repent, and be baptized every one of you in the name of Jesus

Christ for the forgiveness of your sins: and you shall receive the gift of the Holy Spirit" (Ac 2:38).

This Pentecost scene as described in Luke-Acts cannot be understood adequately apart from its reference to the Tower of Babel story in Genesis 11. As described briefly in chapter 2 of this study, the theology of sin's origins as presented in the first part of Genesis culminates in an arrogant attempt to devise a way to enter the heavenly realm regardless of God's wise and loving designs for sharing life in the mystery of divine and human friendship. The Babel story concludes with a picture of a fragmented, dispersed human race, unable to communicate because the language of all the earth became confused (Gn 11:7-9).

When the Pentecost multitude came together, they were utterly amazed and bewildered because they all heard the message of the Holy Spirit in their own language. Coming "from every nation under heaven" (Ac 2:5) they testified, "we hear them telling in our own tongues the mighty works of God" (Ac 2:11).

The Pentecost event in Acts 2 is artistically designed to illustrate that the tragedy of human sin in rejecting God's love was being reversed in the process of accepting the Spirit whom Jesus promised to send. A fragmented human family unable to communicate with one another was now experiencing the healing power of God enabling the peoples of the earth to understand one another. In this context it is important to ponder Peter's words encouraging repentance and baptism in the name of Jesus for the forgiveness of sins. Significantly Peter added, "and you shall receive the gift of the Holy Spirit" (Ac 2:38).

Peter's words as indicated in the third chapter of Acts, quite likely an earlier source than chapter 2, give added insight into the early Church's awareness of what Jesus had accomplished in the mystery of his death and resurrection. After curing a cripple at the Beautiful Gate of the temple, Peter addressed the awestruck people. Drawing on covenant and servant theology familiar to his hearers, Peter claimed that "The God of Abraham, and of Isaac, and of Jacob, the God of our fathers, glorified his servant Jesus" (Ac 3:13). As Peter continued to decry the crucifixion, he referred to Jesus as "the Holy and Righteous One" and "the Author of life, whom God raised from the dead" (Ac 3:14, 15).

Peter continued in words reminiscent of the Emmaus account wherein Jesus spoke of the prophet's foretelling that the "Christ should suffer" (Ac 3:17). Peter then mentioned Moses and all the prophets and concluded with a strong proclamation. "You are the sons of the prophets and of the covenant which God gave to your fathers, saying to Abraham, 'And in your posterity shall all the families of the earth be blessed .' God, having raised up his servant, sent him to you first, to bless you in turning every one of you from your wickedness" (Ac 3: 25, 26). Note that Peter proclaimed that all the families of the earth, not only the Jewish people, will be blessed through Jesus' death and resurrection.

Peter suffered arrest as a result of this proclamation. When brought before the high-priestly tribunal, Peter was even more insistent about the universal power of Jesus' death and resurrection. Boldly he asserted "And there is no other name under heaven given among men by which we must be saved" (Ac 4:12).

Peter's remarks were similar on another occasion when he was brought before the high priest. He stated emphatically, "The God of our fathers raised Jesus whom you killed by hanging him on a tree. God exalted him at his right hand as Leader and Savior, to give repentance to Israel and forgiveness of sins" (Ac 5:30, 31). It is most significant that this text gives Jesus the title, Savior.

The Cornelius story as related in Acts 10 includes a sermon of Peter which could be described as a summary of the Gospel. Peter began by attesting once again to God's impartial love for all peoples. "In every nation any one who fears him and does what is right is acceptable to him" (Ac 10:34). Peter went on to describe briefly the remarkable ministry of Jesus, "preaching good news of peace" as "Lord of all" (Ac 10:36), "doing good and healing all that were oppressed by the devil, for God was with him" (Ac 10:38). After emphasizing the tragic death and glorious resurrection of Jesus, including his manifestations to chosen witnesses, Peter resoundingly affirmed the universal power of the risen Jesus as judge of all peoples. Without any hesitation Peter asserted, "And he commanded us to preach to the people, and to testify that he is the one ordained by God to be judge of the living and the dead. To him all the prophets bear witness that every one who believes in him receives forgiveness of sins through his name" (Ac 10:42, 43).

This brief survey of the earliest preaching of the Church as exemplified in Peter's sermons highlights a very significant faith development with respect to understanding who Jesus is and what he had accomplished through his death and resurrection. Fearlessly the disciples gave testimony to their experience of a new mode of presence on the part of the risen Jesus. As they proclaimed the power of God in raising Jesus from the dead, they did so in the context of their own Hebraic understanding of God's fidelity to the covenantal promise made to Abraham, their father in faith. Jesus' resurrection was the ultimate proof that God's offer of covenantal friendship would never be destroyed by human sin.

Jesus' resurrection was also the ultimate proof that God's redeeming love had destroyed the power of death. Jesus' entry into the mystery of death meant human death was transfromed into an experience of new life. When the early Church referred to Jesus as "first-born from the dead" (Col 1:18), Christians proclaimed their faith in the transforming power of the risen Jesus at work in the deaths of his sisters and brothers in the human family of God.

In the first five chapters of Acts which witness to the beginning of Christian life in the Jerusalem community of faith, Jesus is seen as the Isaian Servant of Yahweh (Ac 3:13, 26; 4:28, 31). He was the one over whom Yahweh grieved "because he poured out his soul to death and was numbered with the transgressors" (Is 53:12). He was the one about whom the Gentiles lamented as "a man of sorrows, and acquainted with grief" (Is 53:3), one "wounded for our transgressions" and bruised for our iniquities" (Is 53:5). He was the one to whom Yahweh promised that he would "see the fruit of the travail of his soul and be satisfied" (Is 53:11). To the suffering servant Yahweh pledged a "portion with the great" and "spoil with the strong" (Is 53:12).

Peter's sermons testify that Yahweh's promises to the servant were fulfilled in Jesus. New titles were given to "Jesus of Nazareth, a man attested by God with mighty works and wonders and signs which God did through him" (Ac 2:22). Jesus was called Lord and Christ (Ac 2:36); Holy and Righteous One (Ac 3:14, 15); Author of life (Ac 3:15); Leader, Savior (Ac 5:31); Lord of all (Ac

10:36); judge of the living and dead (Ac 10:43). To Jesus' death and resurrection were attributed universal power (Ac 10:34f.). All people could be "saved through the name of Jesus" (Ac 4:12). Quite clearly, these early sermons illustrate that through the experience of Pentecost, the early Chrstians' faith in Jesus was transformed radically.

In trying to gain insight into the faith understanding of the primitive Church, it is necessary to recall that all the first Christians were Jewish Christians. Their faith understanding was formed in the context of their own Hebraic tradition. For them, servant of Yahweh meant far more than one who serves. For them, covenant meant God's continued faithfulness in saving them from all their enemies (Lk 1:71-74).

The theme of salvation was key in Israel's understanding of God's action in the lives of the chosen people. When Peter called Jesus, Savior, and proclaimed that "there is no other name under heaven... by which we must be saved"(Ac 4:12), Peter spoke from the centuries old tradition of the covenantal God's saving actions.

The eminent scripture scholar, Stanislas Lyonnet, in his study, *Sin, Redemption, and Sacrifice*, devotes the entire second part to *The Terminology of Redemption*. With painstaking care, Lyonnet begins this section with tracing the concept of salvation. His study has been a key source in clarifying scriptural understandings of salvation, liberation, redemption, and expiation.

Lyonnet emphasizes that the origin of the New Testament notion of salvation is found in the Hebrew scriptures and therefore must be understood in that Hebraic frame of reference. He notes an important progression in the faith of Israel with respect to God's saving actions. At first the emphasis was on temporal dangers, the Exodus being the prime example of Yahweh's saving power. Gradually Yahweh's salvation was understood also in the context of spiritual danger or sin.[4] In the promise of a new covenant as proclaimed by the prophet Ezechial, Yahweh definitely is involved in saving Israel from sin. After

---

[4]Stanislas Lyonnet, Leopold Sabourin, *Sin, Redemption, and Sacrifice* tr. Fidelis Buck (Rome: Biblical Institute Press, 1970) p. 69.

promising a new heart and a new spirit, Yahweh says through the prophet, ". . . and you shall be my people, and I will be your God. And I will deliver you from all your uncleannesses" (Ez 36:29).

As Israel's faith developed, salvation became associated with all the blessings which were associated with the Messiah.[5] Salvation for the early Jewish Christians meant that those acts of Jesus which freed people from temporal sufferings and dangers were the beginnings of salvation in the spiritual order as well. Probably those Christians would not describe Jesus' actions in terms of two orders. For them, Jesus' messianic salvation meant the conferring of *shalom*, the fullness of blessings for the whole person, for the whole community and for the whole world. Furthermore, to confer the title Savior on Jesus meant that Jesus' saving actions were understood as Yahweh's saving actions. Here we have one of the earliest expressions of the unique oneness of the divine and human in Jesus.

The concept of salvation in Hebraic thought is aligned closely with that of liberation and redemption, with the securing of freedom from a situation of oppression. For the Israelites the Exodus was their key experience of salvation because it was an experience of God's liberating action. For them salvation had little or no meaning apart from liberation.

This integral relation between liberation and salvation speaks to the mystery of redemption. God's salvific blessings could not be enjoyed by the Hebrews unless God rescued them from the slavery situation of Egypt. God's liberating action had to precede the bestowal of salvific blessings. Historically speaking, the Exodus had to precede the making of the covenant on Sinai. How clearly this twofold action of God is described in the Book of Exodus. God said to Moses, "Say therefore to the people of Israel, "I am the Lord, and I will bring you out from under the burdens of the Egyptians, and I will deliver you from their bondage, and I will redeem you with an outstretched arm and with great acts of judgment, and I will take you for my people, and I will be your God, and you shall know that I am the Lord your God, who has brought you out from under the burdens of

[5]*Ibid.*

the Egyptians' " (Ex 6:6, 7).

Before considering other theological understandings of God's liberating, covenantal actions in the history of Israel, it seems wise to stress the societal situation out of which the Hebrew people were rescued. In more contemporary language, the slavery conditions of Egypt could be described as a sinful situation. An entire people were held in bondage by a societal structure which demanded the existence of an oppressed group. Such a structure is one of systemic evil, that is, the evil is embedded in the system itself.

Today it is of crucial importance to understand salvation in this wholistic context, including the societal order. Far too often, there has been a tendency on the part of some Christians to emphasize a kind of spiritual salvation totally divorced from salvation in the temporal order. It should not be surprising, therefore, that today's liberation theologies rely heavily on the Exodus as a paradigmatic event. Those theologies are developing from the faith insights of oppressed peoples who know first hand the dire need for liberation from situations of social sin. In their emphasis on salvation as necessarily including liberation from sinful structures, today's liberation theologies resonate with a sound biblical theology.

Perhaps Peter's early kerygmatic proclamation in Acts 3 can be particularly helpful in illustrating the intrinsic relation between God's liberating and salvific action in Jesus. There Peter not only referred to the God of Abraham, Isaac and Jacob in the context of the Abrahamic covenant (Ac 3:13, 25), but he also spoke of Moses, thereby indirectly recalling the Exodus. Peter was also very explicit about the need for repentance so that God's salvific blessings could come to a people freed from sin. Peter urged, "Repent therefore, and turn again, that your sins may be blotted out, that times of refreshing may come from the presence of the Lord..." (Ac 3:19).

The Hebraic understanding of God's liberating action is so closely related to the notion of redemption that the two concepts may be used interchangeably at times.[6] However, because the

[6]*Ibid.*, p. 79f.

word redemption can carry certain connotations of purchasing liberty for slaves, great care must be taken to avoid serious misunderstandings about God when the notion of redemption is used to describe God's salvific action in Jesus. It was never intended that God be cast in the role of a slaveholder who demanded the price of Jesus' crucifixion to free the human family held in the bondage of sin. As Lyonnet points out, the New Testament writers preferred the Greek word, *lutron*, and its various derivations to describe liberation or redemption from sin. This word did not imply payments to emancipate slaves.[7]

Closely associated with the Hebraic notion of redemption are the Semitic practices associated with the *goél,* the next of kin. According to their legal codes, the next of kin assumed responsibilities for keeping the property of the clan or tribe intact; for insuring offspring in the case of a relative's untimely death; and for avenging murder, if need be. The *goél* was considered to be a redeemer of family rights.

When the notion of redeemer began to be applied to Jesus, the concept of *goél* had some role to play. Primarily the understanding was a positive one and focused on the matter of kinship. Jesus was seen as redeeming other members of God's family from a situation of sin to one of new covenantal friendship with God.

Sometimes the redeeming action of Jesus was understood in the context of ransom. One of the clearest texts in this regard is found in the First Letter to Timothy. "For there is one God, and there is one mediator between God and men, the man Christ Jesus, who gave himself as a ransom for all, the testimony to which was borne at the proper time" (1 Tm 2:5, 6). As Lyonnet indicates, this understanding of Jesus' redeeming action relies closely on the fourth song of Isaiah's suffering servant.[8] There the Gentiles ponder the servant who made himself an offering for sin (Is 53:10).

But in this context of the suffering servant, as in all others concerning the suffering and death of Jesus, this offering of

[7]*Ibid.,* p. 95.
[8]*Ibid.,* p. 100.

himself must be understood in the context of a complete out-pouring of love. Whatever theological understanding is brought to bear on the mystery of Jesus' passion, death and resurrection, great care must be taken to avoid an interpretation which suggests God is demanding the price of Jesus' life-blood. Such an interpretation is an horrendous distortion of God, of Jesus, and of the whole mystery of redemption.

However, the fact that Jesus shed his blood on the cross did have profound meaning for those early Jewish Christians. Blood symbolism was very precious to them because it meant life itself. In the synoptic accounts of the institution of the eucharist, most explicitly in Mark and in Matthew, Jesus refers to the new covenant in his blood (Mk 14:24; Mt 26:28; Lk 22:30). Such a statement on the part of Jesus obviously was meant to recall the blood ritual which sealed the making of the Sinai covenant (Ex 24:6-8).

There Moses took the blood of the sacrificed peace offerings of oxen and threw half of it against the altar which symbolized God's special presence. Then Moses sprinkled the people with the sacrificial blood after they had listened to the book of the covenant and had agreed to live accordingly. This blood ritual clearly meant a sharing of life between Yahweh and the cove-nanted people. Yahweh and Israel were joined in the bonds of friendship symbolized by the sharing of the same life-blood.[9]

Jesus' eucharistic words and actions, culminating on Calvary, were gradually understood as the sacrificial act of love establishing the new covenant between God and the entire human family, a new covenant which could never be undone. God's own life-blood in Jesus sealed the covenantal friendship bond with the whole human family forever.

The Pauline theology of Ephesians expresses this mystery of new covenant in Jesus' blood explicitly in terms of reconciliation (Eph 2:11f). This Ephesians text speaks of the reconciliation of Jews and Gentiles, that is, all the other peoples of God's world, those who had been "strangers to the covenants of promise, having

---

[9]*Ibid.*, p. 172.

no hope and without God in the world"(Eph 2:12). Then the text is most explicit about the reconciling power of the blood of Jesus in establishing a new covenantal relation with God and consequently with the whole family of God. In Christ Jesus, those who were far off have been brought near in his blood (Eph 2:13). Very significantly, in the context of shedding his blood, Jesus is called "our peace, who has made us both one, and has broken down the dividing wall of hostility" (Eph 2:14).

In elaborating this reconciling action of Jesus, Ephesians speaks of the new person (the new humanity) which Jesus forms, one human family reconciled now "to God in one body through the cross, thereby bringing the hostility to an end"(Eph 2:15, 16). Surely this reconciliation theme pertains to the forgiveness of sins, the reason given for the pouring out of Jesus' blood of the new covenant, according to the Matthean eucharistic account (Mt 26:28). Ephesians emphasizes that the redemptive, reconciling action of Jesus in liberating people from divisive hostility, also means the gifting of *shalom*. Jesus who is our peace came and preached peace to everyone, to those who were far off and to those who were near (Eph 2:17). These profound salvific blessings culminate in a wondrous union with the Christian triune God. Through Jesus, "we both (the entire human family) have access in one Spirit to the Father" (Eph 2:28). It should not be surprising that this Ephesians passage is a key scriptural reference in the US Catholic bishops' historic pastoral letter, *The Challenge of Peace*.

Another Pauline theological theme which gives evidence of the early Church's growing understanding of the universal significance of Jesus' passion, death and resurrection is that of Christ as the new Adam. Paul develops this theme most extensively in the Epistle to the Romans. In the parallelism used to contrast Adam, the one who brought sin and death into the world, Jesus is hailed as the one who brought grace and life.

Schoonenberg reminds us that the theology of the fifth chapter of Romans was written primarily in praise of salvation.[10] The chapter begins by proclaiming our justification by faith and then

[10]Schoonenberg, p. 129.

proceeds to acclaim the peace with God which we enjoy through our Lord Jesus Christ (Rm 5:1). Paul attributes our justification to the shedding of Jesus' blood (Rm 5:9). Paul goes on to explain how the wonders of our reconciliation are a cause for great rejoicing. "For if while we were enemies we were reconciled to God by the death of his Son, much more, now that we are reconciled, shall we be saved by his life. Not only so, but we also rejoice in God through our Lord Jesus Christ, through whom we have now received our reconciliation" (Rm 5:10, 11). All this has happened because of God's unbelievable love for us (Rm 5:8). This love will bring us to "eternal life through Jesus Christ our Lord" (Rm 5:21).

As the early Church moved more and more into the Gentile world, other theological attempts were made to give new understanding to the mystery of Jesus' salvific death and resurrection. One of the great theological works of the post-apostolic period was that of St. Irenaeus of Lyon who wrote at the end of the second century. In his *Proof of the Apostolic Preaching*, Irenaeus developed the theory of recapitulation as begun in Paul's new Adam theology.

For Irenaeus, Christ as the new head of the human family restored everything Adam lost. According to Irenaeus, in the mystery of the incarnation, Jesus restored God's original plan for the human race. Most basically Jesus restored communion between God and the human family. With considerable detail, Irenaeus expounded incident after incident in salvation history up to the time of Jesus, and explained how Jesus either reversed human responses rejecting God's covenantal design, or fulfilled the covenantal promises spoken by Israel's prophets and other spiritual leaders.

Irenaeus' masterful synthesis of Jesus' recapitulating actions represents a bridging of two cultural understandings, the Hebraic and the Greek. Throughout those early centuries of the Church's life, continual attempts were made to translate the Hebraic thought world into that of the Greeks and the Romans. The Christian conviction of the universality of Jesus' salvific teachings and actions made such "translation" efforts absolutely necessary on the part of the Church's theologians. However, such theological work always involved the risk of losing sight of the basic meanings characteristic of the early Jewish Christian ways of interpreting the mystery of God's love in Jesus. There was always the danger of misinterpreting some of the scriptural under-standings by reading other cultural interpretations into the sym-bolism and verbal expressions familiar to the primitive Church.

A careful analysis of all the theological attempts to clarify the mystery of Jesus' life, death and resurrection is beyond the scope of this present study. One such attempt from the medieval world will be treated briefly, because the explanations of this theological position often have been a source of considerable misunder-standing regarding God's goodness and love.

In the twelfth century, St. Anselm of Canterbury wrote his classic work, *Cur Deus Homo?*, *Why the God Man?*. Anselm used imagery from his feudal society to help explain why the world's need for redemption necessitated the incarnation of God's only-begotten Son.

In feudal society, if one of noble rank were offended in some way by a serf of the lower class, only some nobleman could attempt to make amends for the serf. In similar fashion, Anselm argued, the offense of the human family was against an infinite creator God. Human creatures couldn't possibly make amends in a fitting way to the creator of the universe. Consequently, God became human in the mystery of Jesus who, by his suffering and death satisfied the obligations owed to an offended God.

Although there is great logic in Anselm's theory of relating the need for redemption to the mystery of the incarnation, there is also an inherent problem with respect to God's image in this feudal interpretation. Following Anselm's line of thought, one can imagine God in feudal categories, demanding the crucifixion of Jesus in order that the divine honor be repaired in a suitable way. Such an image of a relentlessly demanding God is a far cry from the covenantal God of Jesus who sent him into the world of human suffering and sin to transform it through compassion-ate love.

Furthermore, in many respects, Anselm's explanation moves Jesus' suffering and death somewhat outside of human history. That is to say, the concrete historical reasons for which Jesus was crucified as a criminal can be bypassed in this kind of theological approach. Instead, some eternal design can be construed which mitigates, if not totally ignores the real life situations responsible for Jesus' death. Such an ahistorical mentality also can ignore quite readily the sinful situations causing the sufferings and deaths of many Christians throughout the centuries including our own.

Today's liberation theologians are adamant in their insistence on emphasizing the immediate historical factors responsible for the death of Jesus. For the most part, these theologians are writing from the perspective of a martyrdom Church, one which knows continual persecution because of its faith and trust in Jesus. Sobrino in particular stresses the fact that genuine theological insight can come only from praxis—the following of Jesus which inserts one into the mystery of his way of life-giving love even unto death.

In the following of Jesus, today's Christians all over the world are learning anew one of the most precious faith insights of the early Church, as expressed in Paul's letter to the Philippians. As a prisoner Paul wrote about the surpassing worth of knowing Christ Jesus his Lord (Ph 3:8). Paul pleaded, "that I may know him and the power of his resurrection, and may share his sufferings, becoming like him in his death, that if possible I may attain the resurrection from the dead" (Ph 3:10,11).

Whatever be the ravages of sin and all the suffering caused by it in one way or another, Christians who have shared the mystery of Jesus' suffering in love have begun to know "the power flowing from his resurrection." Living in union with the risen Jesus has always meant a destruction of the power of sin, along with an experience of trust in the power of suffering in love even through the mystery of death.

As Christian faith matured, the conviction became strong that Jesus became one of us to share all of human life, its struggles and sufferings as well as its joys. That sharing of life was a mutual sharing which continued on in all those who were baptized into Jesus' death and resurrection. Such a wondrous ongoing sharing of life could hardly be expressed adequately in human language. Vine and branches (Jn 15:1f.), body of Christ (1 Cor 12:12f.), holy temple in the Lord (Eph 2:19f.) were some of the earliest attempts at describing the experience of intimate friendship with the risen Jesus. Such mysterious sharing of life in Christ made Paul exclaim, "I have been crucified with Christ; it is no longer I who live, but Christ who lives in me; and the life I now live in the flesh I live by faith in the Son of God, who loved me and gave himself for me" (Gal 2:20).

This life of faith in the "Son of God who loved me and gave himself for me" continues to inspire Christians to live in confident hope that the redeeming love of Jesus continues on in their own lives. For anyone to claim honestly, "Now I rejoice in my sufferings for your sake, and in my flesh I complete what is lacking in Christ's afflictions for the sake of his body, that is, the church" (Col 1:24), means that one has moved profoundly into the mystery of Christ and the Church. Living in this mystery will be our final theme to explore.

4

In the Mystery of Christ and the Church

Anointed with the Befriending Spirit

The Second Vatican Council entitled the first chapter of *Lumen Gentium*, its *Dogmatic Constitution on the Church*, "The Mystery of the Church." The final chapter of that conciliar document was titled, "The Role of the Blessed Virgin Mary, Mother of God, in the Mystery of Christ and the Church." As these chapter titles suggest, the inner life of the Church is highlighted in this major document of the Council. The very first article insists that the Church exists because it enjoys a special relationship with Christ, a relationship of love which enables one to enjoy intimate union with God. In the words of the Council, "By her relationship with Christ, the Church is a kind of sacrament or sign of intimate union with God, and of the unity of all [humankind]. She is also an instrument for the achievement of such union and unity" (LG 1).

Vatican II's *Pastoral Constitution on the Church, Gaudium et Spes,* often referred to as *The Church in the Modern World,* begins by stressing what genuine oneness in Christ means in everyday life. "The joys and the hopes, the griefs and the anxieties of the [people] of this age, especially those who are poor or in any way afflicted, these too are the joys and hopes, the griefs and anxieties of the followers of Christ. Indeed, nothing genuinely human fails to raise an echo in their hearts" (GS 1). This prefatory section concludes by declaring "the Church seeks but a solitary goal: to carry forward the work of Christ Himself under the lead of the befriending Spirit" (GS 3).

In many respects *Lumen Gentium's* final chapter on Mary can be considered a bridge uniting these two conciliar documents on the Church. There are some obvious reasons why the conciliar teaching on Mary can help today's Christians understand better how the mystery of Christ is to be lived in the modern world. With the exception of Jesus, no other person knew quite so profoundly as Mary did, just what the "befriending Spirit" of God can mean in one's life. Because of God's befriending Spirit, Mary enjoyed a unique relation to Jesus. Through the action of the same Holy Spirit Mary continues to enjoy a unique role in the mystery of Christ and the Church.

The theology of Luke-Acts helps clarify this essential role of God's befriending Spirit in Mary's life. In the annunciation account (Lk 1:26-38), in response to her bewilderment over the conception of Jesus, Mary was told, "The Holy Spirit will come upon you, and the power of the Most High will overshadow you" (Lk 1:35). In the days preceding the coming of the same Holy Spirit on the first Pentecost, Mary is singled out in the group of disciples devoting themselves to prayer (Ac 1:14).

In our own times, designated by Pope John XXIII as one of "New Pentecost," as we follow the lead of *Lumen Gentium* with respect to Mary, we will better understand how Mary is with us in the mystery of Christ and the Church. As Christians in the modern world, we can turn to Mary, the first disciple of Jesus, to see more clearly just what it means "to carry forward the work of Christ Himself under the lead of the befriending Spirit" (GS 3).

To speak of the Holy Spirit as the befriending Spirit of God is to use a title which has not been used frequently in the history of the Church. But when one considers the emphasis of friendship in this study, this Vatican II description of the Holy Spirit as befriending is highly significant. To befriend means simply to act as a friend, as one who loves genuinely, who shares life in all circumstances and situations. In this title the Holy Spirit's role in the trinitarian personal life of God is designated clearly as that of bringing us into the enjoyment of God's own friendship. Pondering the meaning of befriending Spirit can give helpful insight into the meaning of the title, Christian, given in the earliest days of the Church's life to those who live in the mystery of Christ (Ac 11:26). The Greek word, *Christos*, is a translation of the Hebrew word, *Messiah*, meaning the Anointed One. In the history of Israel, those who were called to be great friends of God in leadership roles were anointed. The religious ritual of bodily anointing with oil symbolized the interior anointing by Yahweh's own Spirit. To be anointed meant to be touched deeply within by the Spirit of God. All the natural consequences of anointings-- strengthening, beautifying, healing, etc., were transferred to the realm of the spirit. Receiving the touch of God's own spirit meant someone was truly a friend of God, so much so, that God's befriending action could be carried out through that anointed person.

Here it might be helpful to recall once again that Nazareth synagogue scene as described in Luke's fourth chapter. That sabbath day, Jesus began his preaching with an Isaian text, "The Spirit of the Lord is upon me, because he has anointed me to preach good news to the poor . . . " (Lk 4:18). There as he began his public life, Jesus indicated that his entire ministry to all those in need would be directed by the Holy Spirit.

Mary received a unique anointing of God's befriending Spirit when she became the mother of Jesus. Through the anointing of God's befriending Spirit on Pentecost, the Church was formed. From that day forward, other persons have become Christians through the anointing of God's befriending Spirit in the sacrament of baptism. Each and all of these anointings unite one to Jesus in such a way that the mission of Jesus is continued through those who are his anointed friends. To be anointed with the befriending Spirit of God means one begins to live in the mystery of Christ, the Anointed One, who is truly the savior of the world.

Those who live in the mystery of Christ and the Church invariably have looked to Mary for inspiration and guidance in learning how to continue the mission of her son. In his recent encyclical on Mary, *Redemptoris Mater*, John Paul II wrote, "we Christians... feel the need to emphasize the unique presence of the mother of Christ in history . . . (RM 3). The same section speaks of God associating Mary "with the plan of salvation embracing the whole history of humanity."

Right from the beginning of Jesus' public ministry Mary is found in the midst of his followers. The synoptic texts highlighting this fact are being emphasized by contemporary scripture scholars because of their significance for Mary and for all disciples of Jesus (Mk 3:31-35; Mt 12: 46-50; Lk 8:19-21). The various settings are important to study.

In the Marcan account, Jesus is so busy with the needy crowds that he hardly has time to eat. The scribes are arguing about the source of Jesus' power in casting out devils. Matthew presents Jesus speaking to the people about the relentless efforts of an unclean spirit. Luke relates Jesus' parables about the sower and warns about covering a lighted lamp. All three Gospels take special note of the large crowds around Jesus, thereby preventing his mother and brothers from seeing him.

Jesus used the occasion to teach something about the real sharing of life his followers are called to enjoy. They will know the intimacy of family life, a special experience of friendship, if they "hear the word of God and do it" (Lk 8:21). Mark concludes the episode with Jesus' words, "Whoever does the will of God is my brother and sister, and mother" (Mk 3:35).

Although these texts portray Mary as one of Jesus' close followers and earliest disciples, the theological significance of the familial relationship all disciples enjoy is key in penetrating the meaning of Jesus' teaching here. Mary enjoys this familial relationship in a unique way, not because of her physical motherhood, but because of her undaunted faith in Jesus. As we know from the Gospel, hers was a faith like that of her son, who hoped against hope and trusted against trust. As such, Mary's faith and trust witnessed to the redeeming power of God at work in the world, undoing the powers of evil and restoring genuine friendship with God. Mary's faith and trust point the way for Christians of all ages in their efforts to continue the redeeming mission of Jesus.

Recent teachings on Mary continue to emphasize the power of her faith. *Redemptoris Mater* could be subtitled, "Mary's Pilgrimage of Faith." The US Catholic bishops' 1973 pastoral letter on Mary was titled, *Behold Your Mother, Woman of Faith*. Like Sobrino's study on the developing faith life of Jesus, these contemporary orientations to Mary's faith life stress her own growth in faith. Perhaps it is her developing life of faith which most authentically makes Mary a follower of Jesus, one who really shared his own life of faith and its power for redeeming the rest of the human family. And surely it is Mary's developing life of faith which makes her one with us in the mystery of Christ and the Church.

However, in emphasizing the power of Mary's faith along with our own, for our present considerations it is of utmost importance to emphasize Mary's trust. As indicated in chapter 2 of this study, lack of trust in God is at the root of all sin. Conversely, genuine trust in God, which is always intrinsic to faith in God, is essential in establishing the relationship of friendship with God for which the human family was created. Genuine trust in God continually undoes the power of sin.

Two scenes of Mary in the Johannine Gospel illustrate her trust in profound ways: Mary at Cana and Mary on Calvary (Jn 2:1-11; 19:25-27). Theologically speaking, the scenes are intrinsically related through reference to the hour of Jesus. At Mary's request the power of Jesus began to be manifest at Cana; on Calvary, when his hour had come, the full manisfestation of his power takes place. In both scenes Mary's trust in Jesus is without question. At Cana Mary's immediate concern was to prevent suffering for the wedding couple. On Calvary Mary shared the sufferings of Jesus as no other person ever could.

Lucan theology makes explicit the reason why Mary was a woman of unbounded trust. Luke-Acts highlights Mary as a woman of prayer. In loving dialog with her God, Mary grew in the relation of covenantal friendship, so much so, that her trust in God never could be shaken. Whether we contemplate Mary at Bethlehem (Lk 2:1-20); at the Jerusalem temple (Lk 2:22-35; 41-51); or in the mystery of Pentecost (Ac 1:12-14), her prayerfulness accounted for her trust in the midst of enormous difficulties and keen suffering.

Twice in the infancy narrative, Luke comments on Mary's prayerfulness. At the time of the shepherd's visit, Luke tells us "Mary kept all these things, pondering them in her heart" (Lk 2:19). Mary suffered greatly in both Jerusalem temple scenes. Simeon described Mary's suffering by using the image of a sword piercing her heart because of the rejection her son would meet. Years later when the young Jesus was found in the temple after three days, Mary, who had undergone unspeakable agony and did not understand Jesus' explanation, "kept all these things in her heart" (Lk 2:51).

Both temple scenes are designed by the Lucan writer to point ahead to the redemptive sufferings of Jesus which Mary would share most intimately. In the theology of Luke-Acts, the explicit references to Mary's prayerfulness sustaining her in trust and love throughout Jesus' entire life are meant to be understood also with respect to the Church's life, particularly in situations of suffering. Not only at the time of the first Pentecost when the infant Church began to experience the demands of faith and trust in the face of persecution, but throughout the entire history of the Church, Mary's prayerfulness has been seen as a unique sharing in the redemptive power of her son.

In this context of prayer it will be helpful to recall one of the contemporary insights regarding the mystery of sin and redemption. When the results of sin are described in terms of dialogical alienation, then prayer takes on a major role in the entire redemptive process. Prayer breaks through the barriers of dialogical alienation, and enables one to enjoy friendship with God. In the mystery of the Church's continuing redeeming action in union with Christ, nothing is more important than prayer. Only through prayer can one grow in the faith and trust necessary to live as a friend of God. Only in prayer can the friends of God see how they are to share God's own life of love in meaningful and effective ways in any period of history.

Once again we can turn to Mary's prayerfulness as indicated in the Lucan Gospel. There we can see how Mary's prayer enabled her to share her son's vision of redemption, of those saving acts of God in the lives of those who were suffering.

The first time Luke mentions Mary's prayerful pondering is after the shepherds came to see Jesus at Bethlehem. Undoubtedly this is a scene which calls for some prayerful pondering. In the annunciation account Mary had been promised great and glorious things about her child. "He will be great, and will be called the Son of the Most High; and the Lord God will give to him the throne of his father David, and he will reign over the house of Jacob for ever; and of his kingdom there will be no end" (Lk 1:32,33). But in sharp contrast to what seemed to be predicted, in Bethlehem Mary not only found herself in the predicament of using a manger for her baby's first cradle, but also of welcoming poor, rugged shepherds as the first visitors.

The Lucan *Magnificat* sheds considerable light on the Bethlehem story. After Mary proclaimed the wonders her Savior God had done for her, she promised that her God's mercy would extend from generation to generation (Lk 1:47-50). Then Mary began to describe some of the human situations which God's mercy would continue to touch. Prevalent conditions of injustice are reversed. The rich are sent away empty, while the hungry are filled with good things (Lk 1:53). The proud and the mighty are put down from their thrones, while those of low degree (shepherds, for example) are exalted (Lk 1:51, 52). How significant that these salvific acts are proclaimed in prayerful praise.

As Christians continued to ponder Mary's prayerful, trusting faith, they grew in the realization that Mary's relation of friendship with God began at the very beginning of her life. Eventually this faith understanding of the Church was referred to as Mary's Immaculate Conception. Because this gift of God to Mary is of key importance in any understanding of the mystery of redemption, a brief consideration of Mary's Immaculate Conception will be treated here.

In my essay on "Mary Immaculate: Woman of Freedom, Patroness of the United States," published in *Mary According to Women*, I presented a brief history of the development of this Marian dogma. Then in light of contempory theological probings into the mystery of original sin, I focused on Mary's inner freedom as a way of understanding the meaning of redemption in her and in ourselves. Karl Rahner, Juan Luis Segundo, Brian McDermott and Roger Haight are but four theologians whose insights into sin, grace, and human freedom are particularly helpful in this regard.[1] Reflecting on their writings led me to the

---

[1]Cf. Carol Frances Jegen, ed., *Mary According to Women* (Kansas City: Sheed & Ward, 1985) pp. 150-152.

conclusion that the gift of Mary's Immaculate Conception is above all, a gift of inner freedom enabling Mary to be totally open to God's love and to respond accordingly. "Mary shows us how a perfectly free person responds to God in love and corresponds with the inner dynamism of her human freedom as it enables her to reach out in love to all of God's creation. In Mary we see most clearly what our own life of love in God is capable of becoming, because the same powerful freeing action of Jesus is operative in us."[2]

During her life on earth, Mary enjoyed friendship with God in a most intimate way because of her oneness with Jesus, and her complete docility to the befriending Spirit. Now, as Mother of the Redeemer, Mary continues to inspire and to guide all those friends of God who carry on her son's struggle to overcome the powers of evil.

A familiar symbol of Mary's Immaculate Conception is based on the Genesis text foretelling of enmity between the serpent, symbolizing the source of evil, and the women and her seed (Gn 3:15). A similar note is sounded in the twelfth chapter of Revelation where we read of a woman clothed with the sun engaged in momentous conflict with a dragon. When the Church applies these texts to Mary, Christians are reminded of her power in the ultimate struggle against sin, that insidious refusal to accept God's offer of friendship. Both texts speak of the ongoing suffering involved in the struggle against evil. Both texts speak of the ultimate triumph of God's love.

Mary is the person who helps us see that redemption really means freely accepting God's offer of friendship. Therein lies the power to live in the mystery of Christ and the Church, continuing the mission of Jesus to take away the sin and suffering of the world. From the early centuries of the Church's life, Mary has been called a type of the Church. That is to say, in Mary we see what the Church is to become through the redemptive love of her son. From her all Christians can learn the prayerfulness along with the faith and trust essential to enjoy God's life, even in the

[2]*Ibid.*, p. 152.

midst of suffering. Mary continues to teach us how to share God's compassionate love in preventing suffering wherever possible. With Mary's unfailing help, Christians continue the redemptive action of Jesus Christ.

Completing What is Lacking

In recent years, largely as a result of an historical consciousness influencing scripture studies, Christians have become increasingly aware of the ongoing nature of salvation history. To speak of ongoing salvation history is to speak of ongoing redemptive history as well. In order to enable the human family to enjoy God's friendship in any period of history, persons must be freed from the power of sin and be healed from its devastating effects. In addition, wherever possible, suffering must be prevented. When it is no longer possible to prevent or avoid suffering, then Christian faith must be brought to bear on suffering's meaning and value in the light of Jesus' suffering, death and resurrection. Redemptive history is ongoing as the risen Jesus in union with his Christians continue to free the human family from suffering and sin.

As indicated in chapter 1 of this study, one of the most profoundly mysterious texts in the entire New Testament which speaks to this mystery of ongoing redemption is found in the first chapter of the Letter to the Colossians. There Paul is presented as claiming, "Now I rejoice in my sufferings for your sake, and in my flesh I complete what is lacking in Christ's afflictions for the sake of his body, that is, the church..." (Col 1:24). Paul boldly asserts that he rejoices in his sufferings because somehow those sufferings complete the redemptive work of Christ.

To make such a claim is to acknowledge that the redemptive work of Christ is somehow continued in those who are one with Christ in the mystery of the Church. One way to try to understand such a mysterious aspect of Christian faith is to consider this text in the light of the dynamics of human friendship. Once again, some simple questions can be asked. Who are those whom any one of us would consider genuine friends? What does it take to call someone a real friend?

The answers to such questions are not too difficult to come by. As indicated previously in chapter 2, I know that my friends are those with whom I really feel at home. We enjoy one another's company. We like to do things together. If more difficult tasks are to be performed, I know which friends I can call on. But the crucial test of genuine friendship comes when suffering enters my life. My dearest friends are those who share that suffering in selfless, generous ways.

Friendship can neither be imposed nor forced, including friendship with God. Mysterious as it may seem at first, the all-powerful God cannot save us without our free response, because our salvation means we become friends of God. But this friendship is so genuine on God's part, that our ongoing participation in the redeeming action of God is included. As friends of God, we are invited to share our compassionate God's own heartache and suffering as we know it in Jesus. Genuine friendship with God couldn't mean anything less. To be friends of God means to help God save the human family, even when that saving action means suffering.

The Letter to the Colossians expresses this truth of ongoing participation in God's redeeming action in the spirit of rejoicing, of rejoicing in sufferings which really complete the redemptive sufferings of Christ. This understanding of ongoing redemption speaks to the mystery of our friendship with God in a most profound sense. The sharing of life involved here can only be understood in the outpouring love of God's befriending Spirit. It is only in that Spirit that one can live joyfully in intimate union with the redeeming Christ, especially when that redeeming action means entering situations of suffering. Above all in suffering situations, does the experience of sharing in the suffering of Christ precede any genuine realization of what that shared suffering means, and how that suffering can possibly be a reason for rejoicing.

Two of the most significant scriptural texts pertaining to the risen Jesus identify him with human persons who are suffering. The last judgment account in Matthew's Gospel can be considered a description of the great heavenly surprise party (Mt 25:31f.). All those who welcomed the stranger; clothed the naked; visited the sick or those in prison; discover, to their great surprise, that in ministering to those who were suffering, they were serving the Son of Man, Jesus himself. Jesus welcomes these blessed ones into his kingdom by explaining, "Truly, I say to you, as you did it to one of the least of these my brethren, you did it to me" (Mt 25:40).

Paul's encounter on the road to Damascus indicates the risen Jesus' identity with another kind of suffering, that of the persecuted (Ac 9:1f.; 22:6f; 26:12f.). In each of the three accounts of this extraordinary meeting with the risen Jesus, Paul reports the answer to his question, "Who are you, Lord?" "I am Jesus, whom you are persecuting" (Ac 9:5; 22:8; 26:15).

If we consider both of these scenes, the last judgment and Paul's Damascus encounter, in the light of the risen Jesus' saving power, then three aspects of his redemptive action become apparent and are seen to be integrally related. First of all, through a special identity with those who suffer, Jesus the redeemer continues to manifest God's compassionate love for suffering persons. Secondly, those who enjoy the salvific blessings of God in response to the invitation, "Come O blessed of my Father" (Mt 25:34), are those who actively shared God's own concern for those who suffer. Thirdly, Jesus' redeeming action undoes human selfishness and sin whenever persons live in ways which prevent and alleviate the suffering of others, rather than inflicting more suffering for whatever reasons.

In the history of Christian spirituality, there has been considerable confusion and serious misunderstanding about the role of suffering in Christian life. Sometimes people have gone so far as to seek suffering for its own sake as a way to sanctity. Certain devotions to the passion of Jesus have been misleading in this regard, along with some penitential practices.

Apparently, similar problems in regard to penitential practices arose in Israel's history also, as we know from the Book of Isaiah (Is 58:1f.). There the prophet minces no words regarding God's ways of redeeming people from their own sinfulness. Crying aloud and lifting his voice like a trumpet, in the name of Israel's God this Isaian prophet declared a message not unlike the dialog in Matthew's judgment scene. After decrying fasting and the wearing of sackcloth and sitting in ashes, while quarreling, fighting and the oppression of workers was blithely going on, the judgment of God was declared about such hypocritical conduct. "Is not this the fast that I choose: to loose the bonds of wickedness, to undo the thongs of the yoke, to let the oppressed go free, and to break every yoke? Is it not to share your bread with the hungry, and bring the homeless poor into your house; when you see the naked, to cover him, and not to hide yourself from your own flesh" (Is 58:6, 7)? Very significantly, the first section of this prophetic proclamation ends with the promise of God's special presence if these acceptable ways of "fasting" are chosen. "Then you shall call, and the Lord will answer; you shall cry, and he will say, Here I am" (Is 58:9).

Once again, in this context of redemptive suffering we face the question of God's image. God is not a god who sends suffering, contrary to what many sincere, devout people have been taught to believe. God, as we know most clearly in Jesus, is concerned about freeing people from suffering, especially the suffering of sin. Whenever Christians, or any other persons of whatever faith, are involved in undoing human suffering, they are acting under the influence of God's befriending Spirit. Such actions may take the form of healing; of comforting; of working to eradicate the causes of suffering; of teaching; of strengthening faith necessary to sustain one in times of unavoidable suffering and find therein meaning and hope.

In this concluding section, I want to concentrate on some aspects of shared redemptive suffering which are prevalent in our times. Similar considerations could be made for any period of Christian history. But we do live in a time of New Pentecost. God's befriending Spirit is exceedingly active in our world, uniting us ever more intimately to the risen Jesus whose redemptive power is at work within us and through us.

From the vantage point of the final decades of the twentieth century, any honest consideration of human suffering readily can become overwhelming. No other century has known such massive sufferings as ours. Continual wars on global scales have meant cruel deaths for millions of people. including noncombatant children, women and men as total war entered human history through aerial bombing. No other century has seen anything like the number of displaced persons and refugees who now roam the face of the earth. The Jewish holocaust will eternally mark the twentieth century as one of attempted extermination of an entire people through perverse use of modern technology. We, the United States, will forever be known as the nation that ushered in the terror of nuclear war. And now there looms on the horizon the real possibility of total destruction of all life on this planet if even part of the presently stock-piled nuclear weapons are used.

In addition to war, but not unrelated to it, are the staggering facts of world hunger, increasing homelessness, international drug traffic, ecological destruction, and all the resulting psychological problems plaguing people of all ages, perhaps youth most of all. These tragic problems of our times compound the perennial problems associated with family breakdown, crime, disease, poverty, and all the systemic injustices caused by sexism and racism in one form or another. Such a focus on the suffering of our twentieth century world continues to raise questions about the reality of Christ's ongoing redemptive action. Who are being redeemed from what? Where is salvation taking place? What does redemption really mean today?

These crucial questions about the reality of redemption could be answered by shifting the focus of concern from time to eternity. The new earth and heaven promised in the Book of Revelation, chapter 21, have not yet arrived, quite obviously. Perhaps we are meant to do nothing more than wait for their coming, in faith and in trust. But such a focus solely on eternity bespeaks the kind of otherworldly spirituality for which the Church has been criticized severely from time to time, and rightly so. Furthermore, an exclusively otherworldly spirituality contradicts Jesus' own active concern for this world's sufferings as well as the active involvement in this world to which his Christians have given witness.

Somehow it always seems easier to keep track of evil happenings in our world than to keep records of all the ways evil acts are being prevented along with the manifold ways human suffering is being alleviated or healed. Each day our media coverage is filled with accounts of evil doings and catastrophes of one form or another. Far less frequent are news stories portraying the countless daily efforts to help those who are suffering and the myriad attempts to create a more just, humane and peaceful world. In those constructive actions for good can be found the empowering of God's befriending Spirit enabling the redemptive action of Jesus to continue.

The history of the Church's social teaching portrays a remarkable development of awareness regarding Christian involvement in the ongoing struggle to bring about situations of justice and peace in this world. True to the witness of Jesus in his constant, active concern for those who were suffering in any way, the early Christian community not only continued the ministry of Jesus in freeing people from ignorance and in healing the sick, but also began to find ways to take care of the material needs of the poor (cf. Ac 2:47; 4:32-35). Centuries of Christian life witness to more and more organized efforts to take care of the sick, the orphan, the ignorant, the elderly, etc. through the Church's hospitals, orphanages, schools and social services of all kinds. It is important to see all of these efforts as part of the ongoing redemptive mission of Jesus. It is also important to realize that all of the daily efforts of women and men in the workplace and in the home contribute to the ongoing work of redemption whenever and wherever compassionate love and care for others is manifest. However, in the twentieth century, in response to the enormity of human suffering, the Church in official teachings has emphasized ministries more directly involved with eradicating the causes of so much human misery. These are the ministries of justice and peace, ministries focused on bringing about systemic change. While such new ministries of justice and peace are developing, the Church also continues the centuries-old efforts at alleviating and healing human hurts of all kinds.

Developing the theology of Vatican II's *Gaudium et Spes*, the 1971 Synod document, *Justice in the World*, voiced this growing emphasis in Catholic social teaching in a remarkable statement: "Action on behalf of justice and participation in the transformation of the world fully appear to us as a constitutive dimension of the preaching of the Gospel, or, in other words, of the Church's mission for the redemption of the human race and its liberation from every oppressive situation" (JW 6). Christians who have taken this statement to heart have known new ways of "completing what is lacking in Christ's afflictions for the sake of his body . . . " (Col 1:24).

Perhaps no group of Christians has taken this teaching more seriously than those in Latin America. Through its action on behalf of justice, spurred on by a preferential option for the poor, today's Church in Latin America has become a martyrdom Church. A similar phenomenon is occurring in the Church of South Africa with its life and death struggle against the scourge of apartheid.

The Church in the United States is becoming more sensitized to the ministry of justice and of peacemaking. The impact of the US Catholic bishops' landmark pastoral letters, *The Challenge of Peace* and *Economic Justice for All* is beginning to make a difference in Christian communities throughout the country. In the peace pastoral, when the bishops emphasize that "peacemaking is not an optional commitment" but a "requirement of our faith," they declare, "We are called to be peacemakers, not by some movement of the moment, but by our Lord Jesus"(CP 333).

In the ministry of peacemaking, Christians all over the world are experiencing sufferings which range from coping with apathy and resistance to facing imprisonment and death in their efforts to curb militarism through active nonviolence. Bernard Häring's recent work, *The Healing Power of Peace and Nonviolence* speaks to the salvific role of peacemaking. Häring introduces the final chapter on the Church's role in nonviolent witness by claiming, "The Lord has entrusted to the Church a mission to heal and to reveal the healing power of peace and nonviolence, as an integral part of her mission for salvation and wholeness."[3]

When Monika Hellwig wrote her final chapter in *Jesus The Compassion of God*, she entitled it "Jesus and Gandhi: Salvation and Nonviolence." Her insightful remarks climaxed with the following statement on the power of the risen Jesus made manifest in today's nonviolent efforts. "This is perhaps the

[3]Bernard Häring, *The Healing Power of Peace and Nonviolence* (New York: Paulist, 1986) p. 125.

clearest sign that Christ is risen and is among us, for the incarnate Compassion of God is most appropriately and powerfully expressed in non-violent action for justice and peace in the world."[4]

Today's effort for justice and peace may lead some people to wonder if the Church has not moved from an otherworldly spirituality to one which now focuses exclusively on God's salvific acts in this world. Persons of faith actively involved in ministries of justice and peace would be the first to challenge such a view. First of all, those persons know from experience how much they depend on the continual help of God's befriending Spirit to sustain and direct them in wise strategies and actions for justice and for peacemaking. Secondly, those persons know in faith that the full fruit of their efforts will not be seen until eternity, even though some of their efforts will bear fruit in time. This kind of trust and hope for the future needs constant strengthening in prayer.

Again we can turn to Bernard Häring for words of wisdom in this regard. In his comments on the Church's responsibility to reveal the healing power of nonviolence, Häring reminds us of the necessity of prayer. "Action and prayer must always be joined so that [the Church] may never forget that peace and the strength to choose nonviolence are undeserved gifts of God."[5] In prayer Christians working directly for justice and for peace, along with all other Christians completing Christ's redemptive mission in one way or another, find strength to continue day after day often in the face of seemingly insurmountable obstacles. Above all in prayer Christians know that the fullness of Christ's redemptive action will be manifest only when the new heaven and the new earth do appear. For only then in a definitive way will God "wipe away every tear ... and death shall be no more, neither shall there be mourning nor crying nor pain anymore, for the former things have passed away" (Rev 21:4).

Proclaiming the Mystery of Faith

As the Book of Revelation comes to a close, it presents this

[4]Monika Hellwig, *Jesus The Compassion of God* (Wilmington: Michael Glazier, 1983) p. 155.

[5]Häring, *The Healing*, p. 125.

image of a compassionate God wiping away every tear and finally destroying death, mourning, crying and pain. In the eucharistic prayer for Masses for the Dead, reference is made to this comforting text as the Church asks God to welcome "all who have left this world in your friendship." Not only in Masses for the Dead, but whenever the third eucharistic prayer is prayed, all those united in worship hear these words:

> Welcome into your kingdom
>   our departed brothers and sisters,
> and all who have left this world
>   in your friendship.
> We hope to enjoy forever
>   the vision of your glory,
> through Christ our Lord,
>   from whom all good things come.

These beautiful liturgical texts, integral to the Church's most solemn moment of prayer, remind us that our friendship with God begins in this world and culminates in the next. Perhaps there is no more profound nor simple way for the Church to proclaim that Jesus, through his life-giving death and resurrection, truly has restored our friendship with God.

When the fourth eucharistic prayer is prayed, Christians hear very explicitly, "we now celebrate this memorial of our redemption, . . . the acceptable sacrifice which brings salvation to the whole world." In this prayer the worshipping community is reminded that even when the human family "lost God's friendship," . . . again and again God offered a covenant. Then the new covenantal actions of Jesus are recalled.

> To the poor he proclaimed
>   the good news of salvation,
> to prisoners, freedom,
> and to those in sorrow, joy.
> In fulfillment of your will
> he gave himself up to death;
> but by rising from the dead,
> he destroyed death and restored life.
> And that we might live no longer

for ourselves but for him,
he sent the Holy Spirit from you,
  Father,
as his first gift to those who believe,
to complete his work on earth
and bring us the fullness of grace.

Day after day, week after week, in her eucharistic worship, the Church witnesses to a most profound teaching of the Second Vatican Council as voiced in the *Constitution on the Sacred Liturgy, Sacrosanctum Concilium.* "The liturgy is the summit toward which the activity of the church is directed; at the same time it is the fountain from which all her power flows (SC 10). To describe the liturgy as the summit of all the Church's activity and the fount of all the Church's power is to place the Church's worship at the very center of Christian life. Above all in the eucharist the Church knows a unique oneness with the risen Jesus in the celebration of the new covenant in his blood. Every other action of the Church in each and all ministries is effective insofar as that action is oriented to the eucharistic action of the risen Jesus.

Could the new covenant be celebrated in any way other than a meal? What sign of friendship is more universally recognized than that of sharing food together? In the eucharist we share food with God and with one another. We share in the very life of God together. We are nourished and strengthened to continue the redemptive mission of Jesus, to "complete his work on earth" as intimate friends of God.

In every eucharist the Church knows that there above all, the redemptive action of Jesus is made present. In every eucharist, the transforming action of God's befriending Spirit enables the mystery of redemption from sin and suffering to continue on in us and through us who rejoice in celebrating our friendship with God. No wonder in the eucharist the Church proclaims joyfully the mystery of faith:

Lord, by your cross and resurrection
you have set us free.
You are the Savior of the world.

Selected Bibliography

Carlo Carretto, *Why O Lord? The Inner Meaning of Suffering* (Maryknoll: Orbis,1986)

A.M. Dubarle, *The Biblical Doctrine of Original Sin* (New York: Herder and Herder, 1964)

Séan Fagan, *Has Sin Changed?* (Wilmington: Michael Glazier, 1977)

Viktor E. Frankl, *Man's Search for Meaning: An introduction to logotherapy* (New York: Washington Square Press, 1971)

Albert Gelin, Albert Descamps, *Sin in the Bible* (New York: Desclée, 1964)

Bernard Häring, *The Healing Power of Peace and Nonviolence* (New York: Paulist,1986)

_____, *Sin in the Secular Age* (Garden City: Doubleday,

Monika K. Hellwig, *Jesus The Compassion of God* (Wilmington: Michael Glazier, 1983)

Carol Frances Jegen, *Jesus the Peacemaker* (Kansas City: Sheed & Ward, 1986)

_____, ed., *Mary According to Women* (Kansas City: Sheed & Ward, 1985)

John Paul II, *Redemptoris Mater: The Mother of the Redeemer* as published in *Origins* 16, n. 43, April 9, 1987.

_____, *Salvifici Doloris: On the Meaning of Human Suffering* (Washington, D.C.: USCC Office of Publishing Services, 1984)

Arthur C. McGill, *Suffering A Test of Theological Method* (Philadelphia: Westminster, 1982)

Lawrence Kohlberg, *The Philosophy of Moral Development*, Vol. 1 (New York: Harper & Row, 1981)

Stanislas Lyonnet, Leopold Sabourin, *Sin, Redemption, and Sacrifice* (Rome: Biblical Institute Press, 1970)

Karl Menninger, *Whatever Became of Sin?* (New York: Hawthorn Books, 1973)

Johann Baptist Metz and Jürgen Moltmann, *Meditations on the Passion* (New York: Paulist, 1979)

Jürgen Moltmann, *The Crucified God* (New York: Harper & Row, 1974)

Piet Schoonenberg, *Man and Sin* (Notre Dame: University of Notre Dame, 1965)

John Shea, *What a Modern Catholic Believes about Sin* (Chicago: Thomas More, 1971)

Jon Sobrino, *Christology at the Crossroads* (Maryknoll: Orbis, 1978)

Dorothy Söelle, *Suffering* (Philadelphia: Fortress, 1975)

Michael J. Taylor, ed., *The Mystery of Sin and Forgiveness* (Staten Island: Alba House, 1971)

_____, ed., *The Mystery of Suffering and Death* (Staten Island: Alba House, 1973)

Jerome Theison, *Community and Disunity: Symbols of Grace and Sin* (Collegeville: St. John's University, 1985)

Francois Varillon, *The Humility and Suffering of God* (Staten Island: Alba House, 1983)

Walter Abbott, ed., *The Documents of Vatican Two* (New York: America Press, 1966)

The Challenge of Peace: God's Promise and Our Response (Washington, D.C.: NCCB/USCC, 1983)

Economic Justice for All (Washington, D.C.: NCCB/USCC, 1986)

Justice in the World as printed in Joseph Gremillion, *The Gospel of Peace and Justice* (Maryknoll: Orbis, 1975)

Chicago Studies 23, n. 3, November, 1984, *A Time for Healing*

Listening 22, n.2, Spring, 1987, *Arts of Suffering and Healing*